the Cook Book

For Ella and Paddy who inspire us every day.
And for all of their generation—may good
food bring joy throughout your lives.

Paul + Alison Lindley

An Hachette UK Company
www.hachette.co.uk

First published in Great Britain in 2013 by
Hamlyn, a division of Octopus Publishing Group Ltd
Endeavour House, 189 Shaftesbury Avenue
London, WC2H 8JY
www.octopusbooksusa.com

Copyright © Octopus Publishing Group Ltd 2013
Text copyright © Ella's Kitchen (Brands) Limited 2013
Photography copyright © Octopus Publishing
Group Ltd 2013
Illustrations copyright © Ella's Kitchen (Brands)
Limited 2013

Distributed in the US by
Hachette Book Group USA
237 Park Avenue, New York NY 10017 USA

Distributed in Canada by
Canadian Manda Group
165 Dufferin Street, Toronto, Ontario, Canada M6K 3H6

ISBN 978-0-600-62675-6

Typeset in Cooper Light and Ella's Kitchen
Printed and bound in Italy

Created by Ella's Kitchen and Harris + Wilson

10 9 8 7 6 5 4 3 2 1

Design and styling: Anita Mangan
Photographer: Jonathan Cherry
Managing editor: Judy Barratt
Design assistant: Abigail Read
Assistant production manager: Lucy Carter
Food stylist: Vicki Savage
Recipe testing: Emma Jane Frost

Disclaimer

A few recipes include nuts and nut derivatives. Anyone
with a known nut allergy must avoid these. Children
under the age of 3 with a family history of nut allergy,
asthma, eczema, or any type of allergy are also advised
to avoid eating dishes that contain nuts.

Some recipes contain honey. It is advised not to feed
honey to children under 12 months old.

Every care should be taken when cooking with and for
children. Neither the author, the contributors, nor the
publisher can accept any liability for any consequences
arising from the use of this book, or the
information contained herein.

Publisher's notes

Standard level kitchen spoon and cup
measurements are used in the recipe.

Ovens should be preheated to the specified
temperature. If using a convection oven, follow
the manufacturer's instructions for adjusting the
time and temperature.

Large eggs have been used throughout, unless
otherwise specified. Herbs are fresh, unless
otherwise specified. Use low-sodium stock, and
avoid adding salt to recipes altogether.

the Cook Book

100 yummy recipes to inspire big and little cooks

hamlyn

Contents

Foreword by Ella's dad

My wife Alison and I became first-time parents when our daughter Ella was born. The new responsibility, the sense of fulfillment and the unlimited outpouring of love are—I'm sure—felt by virtually every new parent. Parenthood really is a life-changing event. By the time our son Paddy was born, I'd been an active father for three years—and I loved it.

I experienced firsthand the challenges of weaning and the issues involved with introducing two babies (and then toddlers) to new foods. Ella, like the vast majority of little ones, was selective about what she wanted to try, often with no consistency from one day to the next. My solution was to do what I do best: to be silly and childlike. I thought up food-based games. I tried to encourage her to look at her food, and to touch it, smell it, and even listen to it before finally eating it. I invented stories and made up songs; I created imaginary friends and performed "magic." I turned mealtimes into events that were messy, noisy, and interactive. Ella laughed and I laughed. Best of all, Ella showed willingness to experiment with and enjoy her food. My efforts worked with Paddy, too.

Then, I had my "lightbulb" moment: healthy food could be—and should be—fun for young kids. This single notion was to be the inspiration for Ella's Kitchen. I gave up my job and set about creating a range of foods for babies, toddlers, and young children. I wanted to develop a brand that would bring together three elements that often work against each other in prepared children's food: healthiness, handiness, and fun.

At Ella's we always try to look at life from a child's point of view—with an open mind and with all our senses. My strong belief is that the more a young child is involved with his or her food—whether that's choosing it, preparing it, playing with it, or eating it independently—the more likely he or she is to try it and to go on to enjoy it. With such a positive start, children are far more likely to grow up to have a healthy attitude not just toward mealtimes, but toward their whole diet and overall well-being, too.

We've created this book to build further on the Ella's Kitchen ethos—to help even the youngest of children develop healthy eating habits that will last their lifetime. I hope that it will give you and your family far more than recipes for fantastic children's food. I hope that the shared experience of creating dishes together—from making the shopping list and buying and preparing the ingredients to discovering how they feel and seeing their rainbow of colors—will help to strengthen your bond. The ultimate expression of this bond is when you sit down to eat together with big smiles, enjoying the meal that you have created.

Our Ella's Kitchen family has had plenty of fun experimenting as we've developed the ideas for this book. Now that it has found its way to your family kitchen, I hope that your mealtime experiences are equally as good!

Keep smiling

Paul

Paul, Ella's dad x
Follow me on Twitter: @Paul_Lindley

In Ella's own words

Ever since I was very young, I've loved playing and experimenting with food. Some of my favorite memories are centered around foodie things. One of my earliest recollections of cooking is from when I was about four and my friends and I created a chocolate café, complete with chocolate cookies, chocolate soup, and chocolate milk shake—although I'm pretty sure everything tasted the same!

My favorite school subject is Food Technology—we learn how to cook more independently and how to make more complex dishes. I love coming home from school on Mondays with a freshly made pizza or pasta casserole.

All of my family enjoy creating new meals and our oven is never put to rest. One of my favorite sensations is when I wake up on a Sunday morning to the mouth-watering smell of pancakes, or when I get home from school to the appetizing aroma of dinner. Whether it's curry or roast, my dad always makes sure that our meals are healthy and delicous at the same time. My brother and I are both very involved with the family's cooking and we often take it in turns to make dinner.

Once, for my grandma's birthday, we each cooked a course. My little brother cooked the appetizer; my dad, a side; my mom, the main; and I made dessert. It made my grandma's birthday extra amazingly, superbly special! I think that letting kids get involved with food from a young age and letting them try new, exciting things is very important. I hope you have loads of fun with our cookbook!

Ella x

Ella, now age of 13

Our cookbook

A little about using this book

We hope that this book is far more than just a cookbook. It's about encouraging your children to embark upon a lifetime's adventure with food. As you involve them in every step of the cooking process, you'll help them to develop food confidence. Their curiosity will turn them into excited culinary explorers—they'll want to smell, touch, and taste the ingredients and they'll love how foods transform during cooking. By taking time to follow a recipe together, you are sharing quality time during which you laugh together, enjoy each other's company, *and* make something yummy.

From the beginning

If you're a first-time parent embarking upon weaning, take a look at our simple weaning guide on pages 10–11. Our tips provide the essence of how to introduce an exciting array of foods to your baby from their first mouthfuls. If you have a toddler and a baby and want to make meals that will accommodate both, look out for the easy to "mash up" icon (see opposite), which flags up the recipes that are also great to mash for your tiny family members.

Little helpers

Tots and toddlers make wonderful helpers, and at Ella's we believe that messiness is all part of the fun: there's a lot to stir, mix, squash, pour, squeeze, and decorate. We love it when little fingers are prepared to feel the textures of different foods during the cooking process and then make foods look beautiful on the plate—even if that's just arranging fruit slices in a pattern.

A lot of the recipes have suggestions for how little ones can help; not to mention our inspirational activity pages, which are intended to create general excitement about the world of food.

At the end of the book, there are some handy stickers. You can use them as rewards for your children for great helping or fabulous eating and as markers for their favorite recipes, too.

Saving time

We know you're busy and it's been really important to us that we provide you with recipes that are suitable for your lifestyle. As a result, the dishes are not only nutritious and delicious, they're easy to make. They've all come from parents like you and have been road tested by Ella's Kitchen families, and our friends.

Whenever we can we've included handy hints and shortcuts to help save you time. For example, we've suggested when you could use an Ella's Kitchen pouch as a shortcut for a sauce or to add color. Then, we've included a chapter called "Hurrah for the Weekend," which you can dip into when you have more time to cook as a family.

Sensible shopping lists

All the recipes in the book use healthy ingredients. Our team of nutritionists has selected and approved every one to make sure that you can provide your children with a diet to nourish their growing bodies. We've avoided using sugar and salt whenever the recipe allows, preferring instead to sweeten and season with alternatives, such as honey, maple syrup, herbs, and spices. Whenever you can, use low-sodium or no-salt versions of bouillon cubes, stocks, and other ingredients that might already have salt in them.

We recommend that you use organic foods, especially for the fresh ingredients. We believe that organic farmers produce their foods using the purest farming standards.

We've tried to be sure that the recipes call for ingredients that you can find easily and that your children will be able to identify. All should be available in your local grocery store and you may even already have a lot of them in your pantry.

We believe that to have a truly healthy relationship with food, children should never feel guilty or awkward about anything they eat. Healthy desserts—and treats for special occasions—are fine, and all our sweet recipes minimize the use of refined sugar.

The Ella's Kitchen Foundation

At Ella's Kitchen we want to do our bit to help make a nutritious diet a part of as many children's lives as possible. The Ella's Kitchen Foundation is our charity and, among other projects, it funds innovative academic research to improve knowledge of young children's relationships with food and their attitudes to a healthy diet. Ten percent of our profits from this book will go to the Foundation.

Key to icons

At the top of every recipe you'll find a combination of the following icons to help make cooking for, and with, your little ones as easy as it can be.

makes	serves	serves
6	4	2+2
		adults + kids
How many pieces the recipe makes	How many children the recipe serves	How many adults and children this family recipe serves

prep	cook	
10 minutes	10 minutes	
How long the ingredients take to prepare	How long the recipe takes to cook	Recipes that are easy to mash with a fork for babies over 7 months old

First foods for tiny taste buds

1 When to wean

All babies are different—some may be ready for solid foods earlier than others; and some will take to weaning more quickly than others. However, recommendations are that you wait until your baby reaches 17 weeks of age before beginning weaning and that the best age to start is at around 6 months.

Look for signs that your baby is ready for weaning. Putting everything in his or her mouth is one good sign, as is being able to sit up without support.

2 Ready, steady, go!

Wakey wakey
When you begin weaning, offer food at times when your baby is alert and happy.

Little by little
At the start, try offering food in the middle of or just after your baby's usual milk feed.

Playing with food
Try giving your little one some blanched veggie chunks to play with while he or she is eating. Exploring shapes, colors, textures, and smells helps babies to love new foods.

Baby knows best
Most babies know when they've had enough to eat. If your little one doesn't seem to want anymore, don't force the issue.

Smoothly does it
Smooth purees give the best texture for tiny tummies, so blend up some veggies or fruit with a little of your baby's usual milk. Veggies and hard fruits (such as apples) will need to be peeled, chopped, then steamed or boiled until soft before you blend them; soft fruits (such as bananas) can be blended immediately.

3 Taste explosion

Babies have 30,000 taste buds in their tiny mouths—that's three times more than grown-ups—so new food is big news.

One by one
It's best to give babies individual foods at first so that they can grow accustomed to the different flavors, colors, and textures. To really make tiny taste buds zing, start with more unusual flavors, such as broccoli and cauliflower, and some less sweet fruits, including green apples and pears. Keep introducing colors and flavors until you're cooking up a rainbow of foods.

Week 1: once a day

Build up from 1 spoonful of puree to about 5 spoonfuls per meal by the end of week 1. Try some of these yummy fruit and veg this week:

 Broccoli

 Cauliflower

 Pear

 Spinach

 Green beans

 Cabbage

Week 2: Once or twice a day

Your baby can slurp up about 5 spoonfuls of puree at each meal. Try some of these yummy fruit and veg this week:

 Apple

 Green beans

 Potato

 Spinach

 Carrot

 Parsnip

Week 3: Twice a day

Offer up to 10 spoonfuls at each meal—a feast! Try some of these yummy fruit and veg this week:

 Sweet potato

 Banana

 Broccoli

 Cabbage

 Pear

Blueberries

Apple

Week 4: 2 or 3 times a day

About 10 or more spoonfuls will tingle tiny taste buds at breakfast, lunch, and dinner—let your baby tell you when he or she has had enough. Try some of these yummy fruit and veg this week:

 Carrot

 Broccoli

 Pear

 Banana

 Cauliflower

 Mango

 Apple

Mixing it up

Once your little one has got used to a lot of individual flavors, it's time to make things even more interesting and mix up the tastes in exciting combinations. Here are five delicious flavor combos guaranteed to get tiny taste buds going.

Mango + strawberry + baby cereal
Papaya + sweet potato + pear
Carrot + pea + apple
Blackberry + apple + pear
Mango + apple + lime

From mush to mash + beyond

All babies are different, and they may reach the following stages a bit earlier or later than we've suggested here, but that's totally normal. Remember that a lot of the recipes in this book can be mashed up or blended for babies at Stage 2 onward, too.

Look for the "mash up" icon

4–6 months

How do I eat?
I can move food from side to side in my mouth, using my tongue.

What can I eat?
Smooth puree with no pieces, such as baby cereal and blended up, softly cooked fruit and vegetables.

7–9 months

How do I eat?
I can mush up soft lumps with my tongue and I can grasp finger foods in my hand and put them in my mouth. Let me hold a spoon and I'll try scooping.

What can I eat?
Fork-mashed fruit and veg; soft-cooked ground beef and turkey, and mashed-up lentils and beans. I love soft finger foods, such as slices of melon, peach, and banana, or soft-cooked carrot sticks.

10–12 months

How do I eat?
I can chew! I may have a tooth or two, so I love to munch on larger chunks. Finger foods with a little bite will help to soothe my teething gums.

What can I eat?
Whole peas, beans, and corn kernels, firmer cooked veg, and ground meat, as well as baby rusks and raw vegetable sticks.

Now I am One

How do I eat?
I'm great at munching a lot of new foods with my toothy pegs. I can pick up smaller pieces of food with my pincer grip.

What can I eat?
Softly cooked small chunks of meat; stir-fries with veggie strips; raisins, blueberries, and other whole berries.

Energy needs for tiny ones

Babies need a lot of calories and nutrients to fuel their superfast growth. In fact, per pound of their body weight, they need more calories than you do!

However, your baby's stomach is still tiny and it can't hold a lot of food all at once. From around seven months, it's important to give him or her three meals and two or three nutritious snacks each day, as well as at least 2 cups of his or her usual milk.

> I use up loads of energy because I'm growing fast and learning to roll, crawl, pull myself up, and even take my first tiny steps.

Handy healthy snacks

Try your baby on the following healthy snacks from about 7–9 months old, depending upon when your baby is ready.

- ☺ Pita bread slices with hummus or cream cheese
- ☺ Breadsticks and dips
- ☺ Cubes of cheese
- ☺ Blueberries, raspberries, and sliced grapes
- ☺ Cooked broccoli "trees" and carrot sticks
- ☺ Cooked pasta shapes— try the spinach and tomato varieties to provide some interesting colors

Fruity banana bars

Try these healthy snack bars from 10–12 months old—they are great for little ones on the go.

1. Mash ½ banana and mix it with 3–4 tablespoons fine milled oats.
2. Stir in 2 tablespoons raisins.
3. Form the dough into small bars, adding more oats if you need to make the dough firmer.
4. Place the bars on a lightly greased baking sheet and cook in a preheated oven, at 350°F, for 10–15 minutes, until firm.
5. Let cool and enjoy.

Learning about food

Our research shows that children develop healthier eating habits if they can explore food not just with their mouths and taste buds, but with all their amazing senses. Then, as they get older, you can teach them in the simplest terms how all that delicious goodness is helping them to grow up strong and healthy.

Good in every sense

Even the tiniest tots can learn to appreciate the sights, smells, and textures of their food. As your little one learns to express himself or herself by pulling faces and making sounds and eventually words, he or she will find many ways to tell you what they think. Even if at the start you're doing all the talking, your baby is taking it all in and will respond with delighted coos, squeals—and grimaces!

Play a game of squeezing eyes tight as you present foods with different smells. Older children will be able to describe or even identify them.

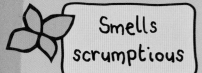

Looks lovely

A lot of different colors and shapes on the plate look more appetizing for little ones. Each time your baby reaches for a food, talk about the color and, when foods are whole, the shapes.

Sounds yummy

What makes an onion sizzle in a pan? How does a carrot stick crunch? How is that different from the crunch of an apple? What's the sound of a smoothie slurp? When we like something, we say "Mmmmm." Encourage your little one to listen to foodie sounds as you cook, eat, and enjoy their meals together.

Tastes terrific

There's no reason why exploring tastes can't become child's play. By Stage 2 of weaning, you can introduce some really zingy flavors. Sit at the table and play a tasting game. Try little pieces of pineapple, or strips of red, green, and yellow bell pepper—any distinctive flavors work really well. Poke out a tongue and give foods an exploratory lick.

Smells scrumptious

Our sense of smell is closely linked to our sense of taste. Encourage your baby to smell his or her food before eating it. Lead the way: Waft it under your own nose and make happy, yummy sounds before you offer it to your baby, who will soon learn to take a sniff and copy what you do.

Feels fine

Allow your baby to pick up his or her food to feel how bumpy, rough, or smooth it is. Again, you do the describing. Remember that babies do a lot of "feeling" with their tongues as well as with their fingers.

Eat a rainbow

Exploring different colors in food is not just about creating excitement—eating all the colors of the rainbow will give your baby the whole spectrum of goodness that he or she needs to grow up great.

Here's our rainbow of favorite foods:

Red: Cherry, cranberry, red bell pepper, radish, raspberry, red onion, strawberry, tomato

Orange: Apricot, butternut squash, carrot, mango, orange, papaya, peach, orange bell pepper, pumpkin, sweet potato

Yellow: Banana, lemon, parsnip, pineapple, starfruit (carambola)

Green: Apple, artichoke, asparagus, broccoli, cabbage, grape, kiwi, lime, pear, spinach, zucchini

Blue: Blueberry

Purple: Beet, blackberry, plum

Color a rainbow! Which colors of fruit and veg has your little one eaten this week? Make a picture using those colors.

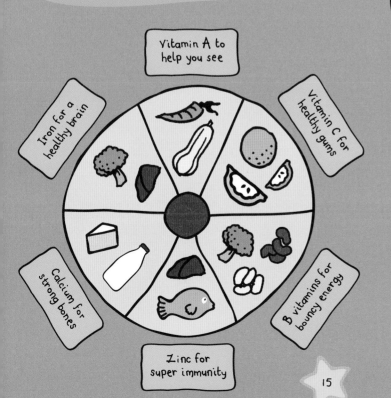

Vitamin A to help you see

Vitamin C for healthy gums

Iron for a healthy brain

B vitamins for bouncy energy

Calcium for strong bones

Zinc for super immunity

The wheel of yummy goodness

It's good to introduce children to the idea that food makes us strong. Use our Wheel of Yummy Goodness as a starting point to teach your toddler about the nutrients that help keep him or her healthy.

yummy lunches + speedy snacks

Have fantastically fruity fun with my veeeery streeeetchy cheese on toast.

Love, Ella x

Beautiful butternut squash soup

serves
4+4
adults + kids

prep
15
minutes

cook
30–40
minutes

This soup hits the spot for a family walk—these children loved it. Perhaps it's the soup's sweet, rich flavor that got their senses going—or the *reeeally* bright orange. Add the cardamom if your little one is up for trying new flavors.

What you need

About 1½ **butternut squash**, cut into 1-inch dice

Olive oil, for roasting

8 **sage** leaves, finely chopped

4 tablespoons **unsalted butter**

1 **onion**, chopped

Seeds from 10 **cardamom pods**, crushed (optional)

4 cups **vegetable stock**

Finely grated rind and juice of 1 **orange**

Crème fraîche or **sour cream** or **Greek yogurt**, to serve

Squashy tasks

Can I help?

Digging out the squash seeds with a spoon is a great way to get children involved in the early stages of the soup, as well as sprinkling the sage before roasting. Ask your little one to watch as you blend the soup—can they see how it changes before their very eyes? However, be careful that the hot liquid doesn't splash.

What to do

1) Preheat the oven to 400°F.

2) Put the squash cubes in a roasting pan, drizzle with a little olive oil, and sprinkle with the chopped sage. Toss the cubes so that they are well coated in the oil, then roast them in the oven for 15–20 minutes or until the cubes are soft and turning golden. Remove the squash from the oven and set aside.

3) Melt the butter in a large saucepan over medium heat, then add the onion and sauté until soft. Add the crushed cardamom pods (if using), the vegetable stock, and the orange rind and juice. Then add the squash. Give it all a stir and bring to a boil. Reduce the heat and simmer for 15–20 minutes, until all the ingredients are soft and pulpy and the liquid has reduced a little. Remove the pan from the heat and use a handheld immersion blender to blend the mixture until smooth.

4) Serve the soup with a dollop of crème fraîche, sour cream, or Greek yogurt.

Cheeky chicken, leek + corn soup

 serves **4**
 prep **7** minutes
 cook **20** minutes

You need just 5 ingredients for this filling and nourishing soup. It's superspeedy to prepare—our Ella's tester had never made soup before and declared this one to be easy as A, B, and C. Your children will love the sweetness of the corn.

What you need

3½ cups **chicken stock**

2 cups **canned corn kernels**

3 **leeks**, finely chopped

1¾ cups **cooked chicken breast** tiny pieces

A small handful of **flat-leaf parsley**, finely chopped, to serve (optional)

What to do

1. Blend ⅔ cup of the stock with half of the corn kernels until smooth, then transfer the puree and the rest of the stock to a saucepan and bring it to a boil.

2. Add the leeks to the stock mixture and lower the heat to simmer for 10 minutes, until the leeks have softened.

3. Add the cooked chicken pieces and the remaining corn kernels to the stock mixture. Simmer for another 4–5 minutes, until the chicken and corn are heated through.

4. Pour the soup into bowls and sprinkle with some freshly chopped parsley to serve (if using).

I'm cheeky

Color me in

Me too!

Veggie-tastic samosas

Easy for tiny hands to grasp and bursting with good stuff, our veggie samosas are a perfect snack served at home, on the go, or in a lunch box. Use our handy folding guide to make beautiful little packages.

What you need

2 cups finely diced **sweet potato**

2 **carrots**, finely diced

¼ cup **frozen peas**, defrosted

1 teaspoon **garam masala**

Lemon juice, to taste

Vegetable oil, for spraying

4 sheets of **phyllo pastry**

Nigella seeds, for sprinkling

What to do

1. Preheat the oven to 350°F.

2. In a skillet, dry-fry the vegetables for 5 minutes over medium heat until slightly softened. Season with the garam masala, and add a squeeze of lemon juice.

3. Spray two sheets of the phyllo pastry with oil and then sandwich them together. Cut the sandwiched sheets into three strips.

4. Blob a spoonful of the vegetable filling at the bottom corner of each strip of pastry. One by one fold the strips as shown in our folding diagram to create three perfectly formed samosas.

5. Repeat steps 3 and 4 for the remaining phyllo sheets, then spray each samosa with a little more oil and sprinkle with nigella seeds.

6. Place the samosas on a baking sheet and cook in the oven for 15–20 minutes or until lightly browned. Serve warm or cold.

Handy samosa folding guide

Cut the phyllo pastry into three equal strips. Put a blob of filling in the bottom corner of each one and fold over and over ...

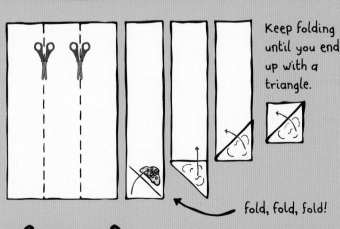

Keep folding until you end up with a triangle.

fold, fold, fold!

Very nice dips for crunchy veg sticks

Fed up with dipping into hummus or mayo? You'll get your little ones happily munching and crunching vegetable sticks all day with these tasty, adventurous dips that are full of complementary flavors and textures. Carrot, celery, cucumber, and bell pepper make the perfect dipping sticks.

Eggplant, pine nut + tomato dip

serves **4** · prep **5** minutes · cook **45** minutes

1 large **eggplant**

3 tablespoons **pine nuts**

2 tablespoons **tomato paste**

1. Preheat the oven to 400°F.

2. Prick the eggplant all over with a fork and put it in the oven; bake it for 45 minutes, until soft. Let cool.

3. In a small skillet, dry-fry the pine nuts until golden.

4. Scoop the eggplant flesh from the skin and place it in a bowl with the pine nuts and tomato paste. Blend to a coarse paste with a handheld immersion blender.

Roast pepper, cream cheese + basil dip

serves **4** · prep **5** minutes · cook **30** minutes

2 **red bell peppers**

1 teaspoon **olive oil**

1 cup **cream cheese**

8 **basil** leaves, finely chopped

1. Preheat the oven to 400°F.

2. Rub the bell peppers with the oil and put them on a baking sheet. Roast the peppers for 30 minutes, until slightly charred, then place them in a large plastic bag and let cool. Peel off the skin and remove the seeds.

3. Place the pepper flesh in a food processor with the cream cheese and blend to a coarse paste. Stir in the basil.

Smoked mackerel dip

serves **4** · prep **5** minutes

2 **smoked mackerel** fillets, skin and bones removed

⅓ cup **low-fat plain yogurt**

1. Place the mackerel and yogurt in a food processor and blend to a coarse paste. Or, if you don't have a processor, use a handheld blender; or flake the fish into a bowl and mash it with a fork, then stir through the yogurt.

Crunchy veggie
dipping sticks

Roast pepper, cream
cheese + basil dip

Eggplant, pine nut
+ tomato dip

Smoked mackerel dip

Veggie fritters

Somehow even the greenest greens taste great mixed with potatoes and these little veggie fritters are a wonderful way to use up some leftover veg.

What you need

2–3 tablespoons **olive oil**

½ **onion**, finely chopped or a couple of **scallions**

4 **russet potatoes**, cooked and mashed

1½ cups chopped, cooked **Brussels sprouts** or **broccoli** or **cabbage**

½ teaspoon **dried mixed herbs** or some fresh **parsley**

2 **eggs**, beaten

Freshly ground **black pepper**, to taste

What to do

1. Heat 1 tablespoon of the oil in a skillet and sauté the onion over low heat for 3–4 minutes, until soft.

2. Put the mashed potatoes and sprouts in a bowl and stir. Add the cooked onion, herbs and eggs, season with black pepper, and mix well.

3. Put another 1 tablespoon of the oil in the skillet and warm over medium heat.

4. Cook spoonfuls of the mixture for about 6–8 minutes, turning once using a spatula, until lightly browned on both sides. (You may need to cook the mixture in batches—using some more oil, if necessary—depending upon the size of your pan.)

5. Serve immediately with a handful of grilled cherry tomatoes and any leftover cold meat you have on hand.

Listen up!

In England, these fritters are called bubble and squeak because the potato and vegetables make popping and squeaking sounds as they cook in the skillet. Ask your little one to listen for them.

Rainbow stir-fry

serves 4 · prep 10 minutes · cook 12 minutes

omit soy sauce

Simple, fresh ingredients in this stir-fry create a colorful lunch or dinner that everyone can enjoy. You don't have to stick to the vegetables we've given here—introduce new ones every time you cook the dish and see if you can make your way through the rainbow.

What you need

2 tablespoons **sunflower oil**

2 skinless, boneless **chicken breasts** (about 10 ounces), cut into strips

1 **carrot**, cut into thick matchsticks

1 **red bell pepper**, cut into thick strips

6 **baby corn**, halved

1 **zucchini**, cut into thick matchsticks

4 **scallions**, cut into 1½-inch lengths

2 tablespoons **tomato paste**

1 tablespoon **soy sauce**

What to do

1. Heat 1 tablespoon of the oil in a large skillet or wok and cook the chicken strips for 4 minutes or until cooked through. Add the carrot, bell pepper, and baby corn, cover, and let cook for 4 minutes.

2. Add the remaining oil, then add the zucchini and scallion and stir-fry for 4 minutes, until the green vegetables are warmed through and the baby corn and chicken are starting to turn golden.

3. Stir in the tomato paste and soy sauce and cook for another 1 minute. Serve immediately—it's delicious on a mound of brown rice.

Eat a rainbow

Ask little ones to identify the colors of the rainbow in the vegetables you're using. What other vegetables would make up the missing colors?

color me in

Quickly does it quiche

serves 2+2 adults + kids · prep 20 minutes · cook 50 minutes

Perfect for a family lunch or a picnic, this easy quiche is quick to make and great for little hands to hold while munching. You could make it ahead and freeze it in single portions, which makes it handy for a lunch or snack on the run.

What you need

1 sheet **rolled dough pie crust**, thawed if frozen

1 tablespoon **sunflower oil**

1 large **onion**, sliced

8 ounces **unsmoked bacon**, coarsely chopped

3 **eggs**, beaten

2 tablespoons finely chopped **parsley** or **thyme**

½ cup **whole milk**

½ cup grated **cheddar cheese**

Go veggie

For a vegetarian option, cook the onion with 3 diced carrots and 2½ cups diced eggplant for 5 minutes. Let cool, then arrange in the bottom of the pastry shell. Pour the milk-and-egg mixture over the filling, sprinkle with the cheddar, then cook as above.

What to do

1. Preheat the oven to 400°F.

2. Roll out the dough on a floured surface and use it to line an 8½-inch round tart pan. Place a piece of scrunched-up parchment paper inside the pastry shell and fill it with some pie weights (or dried beans if you can't get hold of pie weights).

3. Place the pan on a baking sheet and bake in the preheated oven for 10 minutes, until the pastry is just starting to color. Remove the weights and paper and return the pastry to the oven for another 5 minutes, until golden.

4. Meanwhile, heat the oil in a large skillet and sauté the onion and bacon together for 5 minutes, until cooked. In a small bowl, mix together the eggs, herbs and milk.

5. Sprinkle the bacon-and-onion mixture evenly into the baked pastry shell and pour in the milk-and-egg mixture. Sprinkle the cheddar over the filling. Bake in the oven for 25–30 minutes, until golden.

choo choo

31

Great tomato sauce

serves 4 | prep 15 minutes | cook 12 minutes

This sauce is great for two reasons: first, we can think of plenty of ways to use it— see opposite for five of them—and, second, it's packed with veggie goodness.

What you need

1 **carrot**, diced

1 **butternut squash**, diced

⅓ cup **frozen peas**, defrosted

1 (15-ounce) can **baked beans**

1 (14½-ounce) can **diced tomatoes**

2 **tomatoes**, chopped

What to do

1. In a saucepan of boiling water, boil the carrot, squash, and peas for 7–8 minutes, until tender, then drain them and return to the pan. Keeping the pan off the heat, add the baked beans and puree the mixture with a handheld immersion blender until smooth.

2. Return the pan to the heat. Add both the canned and fresh tomatoes and bring everything to a boil. Reduce the heat and simmer for 4–5 minutes, until the fresh tomatoes are soft and pulpy. Remove the pan from the heat and puree again until you have a wonderfully smooth sauce.

Freeze!

This great tomato sauce is perfect for freezing in suitable portion sizes—you'll have a healthy and delicious meal on hand for even the busiest days.

Grow your own

Turn your windowsill into a microleaf garden with edible plants that are quick to grow and delicious to eat. What better way to learn where food comes from?

1

Find your flavors

Arugula, alfalfa basil, and pea shoots all make great microplants—you can harvest their baby leaves within two weeks. Choose some greens you'll use—arugula for pizza, basil for pasta sauce, alfalfa for sandwiches. Yum!

② Paint a flowerpot

Little brown flowerpots are the perfect canvas for tiny-tot decorations. Find some stickers and some paints and get creative. Spots, stripes, or splashes—anything works.

③ Plant the seeds

Fill the flowerpots with damp seed starting mix and sprinkle in some seeds. Sprinkle over a little more mix and place your flowerpots on a sunny windowsill.

Turn your flowerpot into a face with googly eyes and sticker lips, then grow some alfalfa in it. Soon enough your face will have grown green hair!

Tea-set milk pitchers make perfect mini-watering cans for tiny fingers and tiny plants.

④ Harvest the leaves

Remember to talk about the leaves—their color, shape, and smell—as you pick. Use them immediately.

Fantastically fruity cheese on toast

This is a new dimension in cheese on toast that needs both hands to eat it. Teaming up creamy mozzarella with juicy cranberry sauce is just genius. Serve it as a snack at any time of the day (and you'll probably want to eat one yourself).

What you need

2 thick slices **country-style white bread**

Unsalted butter, for spreading

1 tablespoon **cranberry sauce**

1 slice **ham**

2 ounces **mozzarella cheese**, sliced

What to do

1. Lightly butter one side of each slice of bread. Turn one slice unbuttered side up and spread with the cranberry sauce. Top with the ham and slices of mozzarella. Sandwich with the remaining slice of bread, butter side up.

2. Heat a small skillet and dry-fry the sandwich for 2–3 minutes on each side until the bread is golden and the mozzarella has melted. Serve immediately.

Make it streeeetch!

Have a stringy cheese competition. Everyone takes a bite and the one who can make their cheese stretch the farthest is the winner!

Very veggie couscous

There are no fewer than seven fruit and veggies in this delicious meal. The tiny couscous grains and soft consistency make this a great lunch for learning to use a spoon.

What you need

2 **carrots**, finely chopped

2 sweet crisp **apples**, peeled, cored, and chopped

1 cup **couscous**

1 cup **vegetable stock**

1 tablespoon **sunflower oil**

1 **zucchini**, diced

1 **red bell pepper**, diced

4 **scallions**, coarsely chopped

1⅓ cups drained, canned **corn kernels**

⅓ cup **dried apricots**, coarsely chopped

What to do

1. Make a carrot-and-apple puree by steaming the carrot and apple for 8–10 minutes, until tender, then using a handheld immersion blender to puree until smooth. Set aside.

2. Place the couscous in a bowl. In a small saucepan, bring the vegetable stock to a boil. Stir in ½ cup of the carrot-and-apple puree, then pour the mixture over the couscous and cover the bowl with plastic wrap. Let stand for 5 minutes. (You can freeze any leftover puree for use another time.)

3. Meanwhile, heat the oil in a large skillet and cook the remaining vegetables for 5 minutes, until they have softened a little. Stir in the apricots and the couscous mixture and heat through.

4. Serve warm or cold. (You could even serve it warm with some spoonfuls of our Great Tomato Sauce—see page 32—for extra zing, if you like.)

Dig-in grilled tortillas

serves **2** | prep **10** minutes | cook **5** minutes

Wrapping up loads of good stuff in a tortilla and then grilling it in a skillet is a great way to use up leftovers and they are easy for little ones to hold in their hands to eat. Try out different fillings to get their taste buds tingling.

What you need

2 teaspoons **olive oil**, for brushing

2 **flour tortillas**

1 cup grated **cheddar cheese**

⅔ cup small **cooked chicken breast** pieces

2 ounces **ham**, coarsely chopped

2 **scallions**, trimmed and coarsely chopped

2 **mushrooms**, thinly sliced

What to do

1. Lightly brush a large skillet with oil. Lay a tortilla flat in the skillet and arrange half the filling ingredients over half of it, keeping a clear 1¼-inch edge. Fold the empty half of the tortilla over the top.

2. Heat the tortilla over moderate heat for 2–3 minutes, until the cheddar starts to melt. Using two spatulas, carefully turn over the tortilla and cook for another 2 minutes on the other side. Remove the skillet from the heat and slide out the grilled tortilla onto a cutting board. Cut the tortilla into three wedges. Repeat with the other tortilla and remaining ingredients.

Pick me up!

Easy cheesy zucchini frittata

Getting grated zucchini into these frittatas is a simple way to sneak some good-for-you greens into a meal. The frittata is delicious warm or cold and makes a great finger food.

What you need

6 **eggs**

2¼ cups grated **cheddar cheese**, **American cheese**, or **Muenster cheese**

2 **zucchini**, coarsely grated

⅓ cup **raisins** (optional)

3 **scallions**, 1 **leek**, or ½ **white onion**, finely chopped

Small pinch of **chili powder** or **cayenne pepper**

1 tablespoon **olive oil**

What to do

1. Preheat the broiler to medium. Crack the eggs into a large bowl and beat well, using a wire whisk. Add the cheese, zucchini, and raisins (if using), the scallions, leeks, or white onion, and the chili powder or cayenne pepper and beat again to combine.

2. Heat the oil in a 12-inch skillet, then pour in the egg mixture and cook over a gentle heat for 2–3 minutes, until the bottom of the frittata is set. Place the frittata under the broiler and cook for another 3–4 minutes, until the top is set and golden.

3. Slide the frittata out onto a plate and cut into eight wedges. Serve warm or cold with salad.

Go crackers!

Can I help?

Little ones can try cracking the eggs into the bowl and then take a turn at beating them with a fork or wire whisk. Who has the fastest action?

5 ways

Five ways with pita bread, wrap, or roll fillings

Bored with the same old sandwich fillings? These flavor-and-texture combinations put the excitement back into bread—they are delicious, nutritious, and, best of all, interesting.

Chompy cheese, carrot + apple

serves **2**   prep **5** minutes

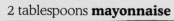

1 tablespoon unsweetened **applesauce** or **apple puree**

⅓ cup **cream cheese**

1 tablespoon **whole milk**

1 small **carrot**, grated

½ cup grated **cheddar cheese** or **American cheese**

¼ sweet, crisp **apple**, grated

2 **pita breads**, toasted

If you're making your own applesauce, peel, core, and chop one crisp apple. Steam it until soft, then mash with a fork.

Blend the cream cheese with the milk, then fold in the applesauce or 1 tablespoon of puree. Stir in the carrot, cheese, and grated apple. Make a slit in the pita breads and fill them with the cheese mixture. Cut each pita bread in half to serve.

Curried chicken + raisins with mango

serves **2**   prep **5** minutes

2 tablespoons **mayonnaise**

2 tablespoons well-chopped **mango**

¼ teaspoon **medium curry powder**

1 cup small **cooked chicken breast** pieces

⅓ cup **golden raisins**

2 **flour tortillas**

2 small handfuls of **arugula**

Use a handheld immersion blender to combine together the mayonnaise, mango, and curry powder, then stir in the chicken and golden raisins.

Spoon half the mixture in a line across the center of one tortilla, then sprinkle with half the arugula and roll up tightly. Repeat for the other tortilla.

Cut each tortilla in half to serve.

Crumbly feta + red grape

⅓ cup crumbled **feta cheese**

¼ cup finely **chopped walnuts**

1 **celery stick**, finely chopped

⅓ cup halved or quartered **seedless red grapes**

2 tablespoons **mayonnaise**

2 **pita breads**, toasted

Fold together all the filling ingredients in a bowl until well combined.

Make a slit in the pita breads and fill with the cheese mixture. Cut each pita bread in half to serve.

Sunshine hummus with basil

1 **clementine**, segmented and chopped

½ cup **hummus**

1 small **carrot**, grated

1 tablespoon shredded **basil** leaves

2 **flour tortillas**

Mix together all the filling ingredients in a bowl until well combined.

Spoon half the mixture in a line across the center of one tortilla and roll the tortilla up tightly. Repeat for the other tortilla.

Cut each tortilla in half to serve.

Terrific tuna with green grapes

1 (5-ounce) can **chunk light tuna** in spring water, drained

¼ cup **Greek yogurt**

⅓ cup halved or quartered **seedless green grapes**

2 **whole-wheat rolls**, halved

Mix together all the filling ingredients in a bowl until well combined.

Pile half the filling into each roll. Cut in half to serve.

Nibbly nacho feast

Children will love to dig in to this crunchy, gooey feast of flavor—all you need is fingers.

What you need

1 (7-ounce) bag **tortilla chips**

½ cup grated **mozzarella cheese**

Lime wedges, to serve (optional)

For the tomato salsa

3 **tomatoes**, chopped

3 **scallions**, finely sliced

Juice of ½ **lime** (reserve the other ½ lime for wedges, if using)

A handful of **cilantro**, coarsely chopped

½ teaspoon **smoked paprika**

For the avocado salsa (guacamole)

1 ripe **avocado**

1 tablespoon **sweet chili dipping sauce**

What to do

1. Preheat the broiler to high.

2. To make the tomato salsa, mix together the tomatoes, scallions, lime juice, cilantro, and smoked paprika. Set aside.

3. To make the guacamole, mash the avocado flesh with the chili sauce. Set aside.

4. Put the tortilla chips on a large heatproof plate and spoon the tomato salsa over them, then sprinkle with the cheese and place them under the preheated broiler for 2–3 minutes, until the cheese has melted.

5. Spoon the guacamole over the top and serve with lime wedges (if using).

Color me in

Dee-licious dinners

How many different vegetables can you name?
Can you get up to 10?

Love, Ella x

Hugely hearty four-bean feast

serves **2+4** adults + kids | prep **10** minutes | cook **35** minutes omit green beans

True to its name, this is a warming feast packed full of delicious flavor, heaps of veggies, and filling, nutritious beans. This is a good one to make for all the family to enjoy.

What you need

1 tablespoon **sunflower oil**

1 **onion**, chopped

1 **carrot**, diced

2 cups ½-inch **butternut squash** dice

1 (15-ounce) can **red kidney beans**, drained and rinsed

1 (15-ounce) can **cannellini beans**, drained and rinsed

1 (15-ounce) can **navy beans**, drained and rinsed

1 (14½-ounce) can **diced tomatoes**

½ cup quartered **green beans**

⅔ cup **vegetable stock**

A handful of **basil** leaves, coarsely torn

What to do

1. Preheat the oven to 400°F.

2. Heat the oil in a large skillet and sauté the onion, carrot, and squash for 5 minutes, until the onion has softened.

3. Add all the canned beans, the tomatoes, and the green beans, then add the vegetable stock and stir to combine. Transfer everything to a casserole dish, cover, and bake for 30 minutes.

4. Stir in the basil and serve with couscous or mashed potatoes.

Tomorrow's lunch

If you have any of your delicious beany stew left over, keep it to spoon onto a hot baked potato, topped with a little cheese; or blend it up to make a yummy lunchtime soup.

Can I help?

Bean prep

Once you've tipped the beans into a strainer to drain them, ask your little one to give you a hand rinsing them through—it's culinary water play!

Ella's dad's sweet + sour shrimp

serves 6 | prep 15 minutes | cook 7 minutes

This recipe from the Lindley family kitchen is a great introduction to the sweet, tangy, savory flavors used in recipes from all over Asia. We've cut the vegetables into strips, but you can slice them any way you like.

What you need

2 tablespoons **sunflower oil**

4 **scallions**, sliced

1 **garlic** clove, sliced

8 ounces **raw jumbo shrimp**

1 **red bell pepper**, halved, seeded, and sliced

12 **baby corn**, halved lengthwise

2 **carrots**, cut into strips

2 **pineapple** slices, cut into chunks

For the sauce

1 tablespoon **light soy sauce**

1 tablespoon **white wine vinegar**

¼ **banana** and ¼ **mango**, mashed together

1 teaspoon **cornstarch**

1 tablespoon **water**

1 tablespoon **ketchup**

1 teaspoon **sweet chili dipping sauce**

What to do

1. First make the sauce: Simply mix together all of the sauce ingredients in a bowl. Set aside.

2. Heat the oil in a wok or large skillet, add the scallions, garlic, and shrimp, and sauté them for 2 minutes over medium heat, stirring continuously, until the shrimp are pink all over.

3. Add the bell pepper, baby corn, and carrots and cook for another 2–3 minutes, until the vegetables are just soft.

4. Add the sauce and the pineapple chunks and stir everything together to combine well.

5. Cook for another 1 minute, until the sauce is bubbling and hot.

6. Serve immediately with noodles or rice.

That's magic!

Encourage your little one to watch the shrimp change color as they cook—as if by magic, their dull gray becomes beautiful pink.

53

Peas please veggie risotto

Risotto is so often a winning formula for tiny taste buds. This pea, leek, and zucchini version is especially easy to put together, but absolutely packed with green-food goodness.

What you need

1 **vegetable bouillon cube**

1 cup **instant long-grain rice**

½ cup **frozen peas**, defrosted

1 tablespoon **olive oil**

1 **leek**, finely chopped

1 **zucchini**, finely chopped

⅔ cup **carrot juice**

cheddar cheese or **American cheese**, grated, to serve

What to do

1. In a large saucepan bring 4 cups of water to a boil. Crumble in the bouillon cube and add the rice. Bring the liquid back to a boil, then reduce the heat to low and simmer, uncovered, for 10–15 minutes, until the rice is tender, adding the peas for the last 5 minutes.

2. Drain the rice-and-pea mixture and set aside.

3. Heat the oil in a large skillet or wok and cook the leek and zucchini for about 5 minutes, stirring occasionally, until softened.

4. Add the rice-and-pea mixture and stir well, then add the carrot juice and continue to cook for another 2 minutes, until piping hot.

5. Serve hot with some grated cheese sprinkled on top.

I love
my greens!

Magical Moroccan-style chicken

serves **4** · prep **15** minutes · cook **25** minutes

This casserole-style dish packs in fruit, vegetables, and beans for an all-round nutritional boost. You could puree it and serve it with baby cereal for very little ones.

What you need

1 tablespoon **sunflower oil**

2 skinless, boneless **chicken breasts** (about 10 ounces), diced

1 large **carrot**, sliced

1 **leek**, sliced

1 **red bell pepper**, chopped

1 teaspoon **ground cumin**

½ teaspoon **ground cinnamon**

1 (15-ounce) can **chickpeas**, drained and rinsed

1 tablespoon **tomato paste**

2½ cups **vegetable stock**

¾ cup **dried apricots**

⅓ cup **dried prunes**

A few **cilantro leaves**, to serve (optional)

What to do

1. Heat the oil in a large saucepan and cook the chicken pieces for 4 minutes, until browned on all sides. Add the vegetables and spices and cook for another 2–3 minutes.

2. Add the chickpeas, tomato paste, vegetable stock, apricots, and prunes and bring to a boil. Then reduce the heat to low, cover, and simmer for 15–20 minutes, stirring occasionally, until all the ingredients are tender.

3. Serve on a bed of couscous sprinkled with the cilantro leaves (if using).

Design your own fez

Tasty turkey + rice packed bell peppers

Cinnamon and raisins give these stuffed bell peppers a hint of Middle Eastern flavor. They are a great way to introduce little ones to sweet spices.

What you need

6 **red bell peppers**

⅓ cup **brown rice**

12 ounces **lean ground turkey**

1 small **onion**, chopped

1 (14½-ounce can) **diced tomatoes**

3 tablespoons **tomato paste**

1 tablespoon **Worcestershire sauce**

⅓ cup **raisins**

½ teaspoon **ground cinnamon**

⅓ cup finely chopped **mozzarella cheese**

What to do

1. Preheat the oven to 350°F. Bring a large saucepan of water to a boil (use enough water to cover the bell peppers). Cut the tops from the bell peppers and discard them, then scoop out the core and seeds. Place the bell peppers into the boiling water, filling their cavities, and cook for 4 minutes, until they begin to soften. Remove the bell peppers from the water, using a slotted spoon (leave the water boiling), and set them aside to drain on paper towels, open end down.

2. Add the rice to the water and cook for 20 minutes, until tender.

3. Meanwhile, place the turkey and onion into a large, heavy skillet and cook over high heat for 8–10 minutes, stirring and breaking up the turkey as much as possible. Add the tomatoes, tomato paste, Worcestershire sauce, raisins, and cinnamon and stir well. Bring to a boil, then reduce the heat and cover and simmer for 5 minutes.

4. Drain the cooked rice, then stir into the meat mixture. Place the bell peppers, open end up, into an ovenproof dish and fill each with with some of the meat mixture. Sprinkle with the mozzarella, then bake in the preheated oven for 15 minutes, until the cheese is golden brown.

5 ways

Five ways with green vegetables

Greens don't have to be boring. We've found the perfect partners for green beans, Brussels sprouts, broccoli, spinach, and zucchini, making the most of all the natural, fresh flavors. High five if your little ones try all five!

Good-for-you green beans

serves 4 | prep 5 minutes | cook 8 minutes

3 cups **fine green beans**, trimmed

2 tablespoons **olive oil**

3 **shallots**, finely chopped

⅓ cup **pine nuts**

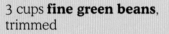

Cook the beans in boiling water for 5 minutes, until just tender, then drain.

Meanwhile, heat the oil in a skillet and sauté the shallots for 2 minutes, add the pine nuts, and sauté for 1–2 minutes. Add the cooked beans and sauté, stirring, for 2–3 minutes to heat through. Serve immediately.

Special sprouts

serves 4 | prep 5 minutes | cook 15 minutes

4 cups **Brussels sprouts**

Unsalted butter, for frying

2 ounces **unsmoked bacon**, chopped

1 **garlic** clove, thinly sliced

1 teaspoon **Worcestershire sauce**

Cook the sprouts in boiling water for 10 minutes, until just tender, then drain.

Heat the butter in a skillet and cook the bacon and garlic for 3 minutes, until browned. Add the sprouts and cook for 1 minute to heat through, then add the Worcestershire sauce and cook, stirring, for a few seconds before serving immediately.

Beautiful broccoli

serves 4 | prep 5 minutes | cook 8 minutes

4 cups **broccoli florets**

1 tablespoon **toasted sesame oil**

1 tablespoon **sesame seeds**

1 tablespoon **light soy sauce**

Cook the broccoli in boiling water for 4–5 minutes, until just tender, then drain.

Heat the oil in a skillet and toast the sesame seeds for 1 minute, until golden. Add the cooked broccoli and the soy sauce and stir-fry, tossing, for 1 minute, until heated through. Serve immediately.

Splendid spinach

serves 4 | prep 5 minutes | cook 5 minutes

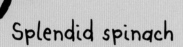

1 (10-ounce) package **frozen chopped spinach**

A pinch of **ground nutmeg**

¼ cup **crème fraîche** or **Greek yogurt**

1 tablespoon grated **Parmesan cheese**

Cook the spinach in a saucepan according to the package directions, drain, and press out as much of the liquid as possible, then return the spinach to the pan.

Add the remaining ingredients and stir to combine. Serve immediately.

Zingy zucchini

serves 4 | prep 5 minutes | cook 7 minutes

1 tablespoon **olive oil**

4 **zucchini**, halved lengthwise and sliced

Finely grated rind and juice of ½ **lemon**

A handful of **basil** leaves, finely chopped

Heat the oil in a skillet and sauté the zucchini for 5–6 minutes, until golden brown and just tender.

Remove from the heat and stir in the lemon rind and juice and the basil. Serve immediately.

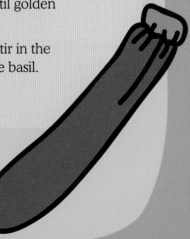

Fish with rice and peas

This wonderful meal introduces kids to fish dishes without a strong smoked-fish flavor, but it has a hint of spice with only a little curry powder (fun for tiny taste buds).

What you need

12 ounces **cod fillet**, skinned

1¼ cups **whole milk**

2 tablespoons **unsalted butter**

1 **onion**, finely chopped

½ teaspoon **cayenne pepper**

1 teaspoon **mild curry powder**

1½ cups **instant long-grain rice**

4 cups **chicken stock** or water

1 cup **peas**, thawed if frozen

1 cup **corn kernels**, thawed if frozen

4 **eggs**, hard-boiled and coarsely chopped

2 tablespoons finely chopped **flat-leaf parsley**

What to do

1. Put the cod in a deep skillet with the milk, bring to a boil, then reduce the heat to low and simmer, uncovered, for 5 minutes, or until cooked through.

2. Using a slotted spoon, transfer the fish to a bowl, reserving the warm milk. Flake the fish with a fork, being careful to remove any bones.

3. Melt the butter in a medium saucepan. Add the onion and cayenne pepper and cook for 2–3 minutes, until the onion is beginning to soften. Add the curry powder and cook for another 1 minute.

4. Add the rice and stir it to coat it in the oil. Pour in the chicken stock and the reserved milk and bring to a boil, then reduce the heat to low, cover, and simmer for 10–15 minutes, until the rice is cooked and almost all the stock and milk have been absorbed. Add the peas and the corn kernels, stir thoroughly, and cook for another 2 minutes.

5. Carefully fold in the flaked fish and eggs. Sprinkle with the chopped parsley.

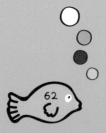

Ella's mom's easy chicken curry

serves **4** · prep **10** minutes · cook **30** minutes

Ella's mom first made this when Ella was just three years old—and Ella has been enjoying it since. It is a mild, sweet, and creamy curry that's guaranteed to get tiny taste buds tingling with all the spices of exotic adventure.

What you need

2 tablespoons **olive oil**

1 small **onion**, chopped

2 **garlic** cloves, crushed

2 skinless, boneless, **chicken breasts** (about 10 ounces), cut into bite-size pieces

¾-inch piece **fresh ginger**, grated

1 teaspoon **mild curry powder**

1 small **sweet potato**, diced

4 **carrots**, sliced

1 cup **coconut milk**

½ cup **vegetable stock**

1 small **mango**, cut into chunks

1¼ cups trimmed **green beans**

2 tablespoons finely chopped **flat-leaf parsley**

What to do

1. Heat the oil in a large saucepan and add the onion and garlic. Sauté for 1 minute, stirring, then add the chicken pieces and cook for 3–4 minutes over medium heat, stirring every now and then until the chicken pieces are golden brown all over.

2. Add the grated ginger and the curry powder and cook for another 1 minute, stirring all the time. Add the sweet potato and carrots, then pour in the coconut milk and stock and add the mango. Mix everything together well and bring the liquid to a boil. Cover, reduce the heat to low, and simmer, stirring occasionally, for 20 minutes, until the sweet potato is soft.

3. Add the beans and cook for another 3 minutes, until the beans are just soft. Finally, stir in the parsley. Serve immediately on a bed of rice or with a pita bread.

Ella's shortcut

To save some time on chopping, you can substitute the chunks of mango for 1 (3¼-ounce) pouch of Ella's Kitchen Smoothie Fruits—The Yellow One.

Color me in

64

Big beef tomato sauce

serves 4 with pasta
prep 10 minutes
cook 30 minutes

This recipe came from a man called Neil who works at Ella's Kitchen selling our food in a lot of countries around the world. He calls it the "perfect pasta partner" and it packs a big taste punch. Go easy on the dried red pepper flakes for very little ones.

What you need

1 tablespoon **olive oil**

½ **onion**, coarsely chopped

1 **garlic** clove, sliced

1 ounce **bacon**, chopped

10 ounces **lean ground beef**

2 cups **tomato puree** or **Great Tomato Sauce** (see page 32)

1 tablespoon **Worcestershire sauce**

1 teaspoon **fennel seeds**

A pinch of **dried red pepper flakes**

A few **basil** leaves, to serve (optional)

Parmesan cheese, grated, to serve (optional)

What to do

1. Heat the oil in a large saucepan and cook the onion and garlic over moderate heat for 3–4 minutes, until beginning to soften. Add the bacon and cook for 3 minutes, until opaque. Add the ground beef and cook for another 5 minutes, until the meat has browned.

2. Pour in the tomato puree or Great Tomato Sauce along with ¼ cup of water. Add the Worcestershire sauce and herbs and spices. Bring the sauce to a boil, then reduce the heat to low, cover, and simmer for 10 minutes; then remove the lid and stir and cook for another 8–10 minutes, until the liquid has reduced by almost half.

3. Serve the meat sauce over cooked pasta and sprinkle with with basil leaves and freshly grated Parmesan (if using).

Beep beep!

Mega macaroni + cheese

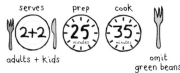

serves **2+2** adults + kids

prep **25** minutes

cook **35** minutes omit green beans

An easy twist on a family favorite, this dish is mega-tasty. The secret lies in the giant pasta tubes, which hold the delicious cheesiness so perfectly.

What you need

9 ounces **large macaroni** or **penne pasta**, dried or fresh

2 tablespoons **unsalted butter**

⅓ cup **all-purpose flour**

2½ cups **whole milk**

1¾ cups grated **cheddar cheese** or **American cheese**

1 teaspoon **English** or **Dijon mustard**

A pinch of **nutmeg**

4 ounces **bacon**, cooked and chopped into pieces

Draw something for the digger to carry

What to do

1. Preheat the oven to 375°F. Bring a large saucepan of lightly salted water to a boil and cook the pasta according to the package directions. Drain and keep warm.

2. Meanwhile, melt the butter in a saucepan, add the flour, stir to combine, and cook for 1 minute.

3. Gradually stir in the milk. Bring to a boil, stirring continuously, until the sauce thickens. Remove from the heat and stir in three-quarters of the cheese and add the mustard, nutmeg, and bacon pieces. Add the pasta to the sauce and stir well.

4. Transfer the mixture to a large ovenproof dish and sprinkle with the remaining cheese.

5. Cook in the preheated oven for 20 minutes, until golden brown.

6. Serve with green beans and a few cooked cherry tomatoes.

More veg!

Make your macaroni and cheese more mega—try adding some of these veggies.

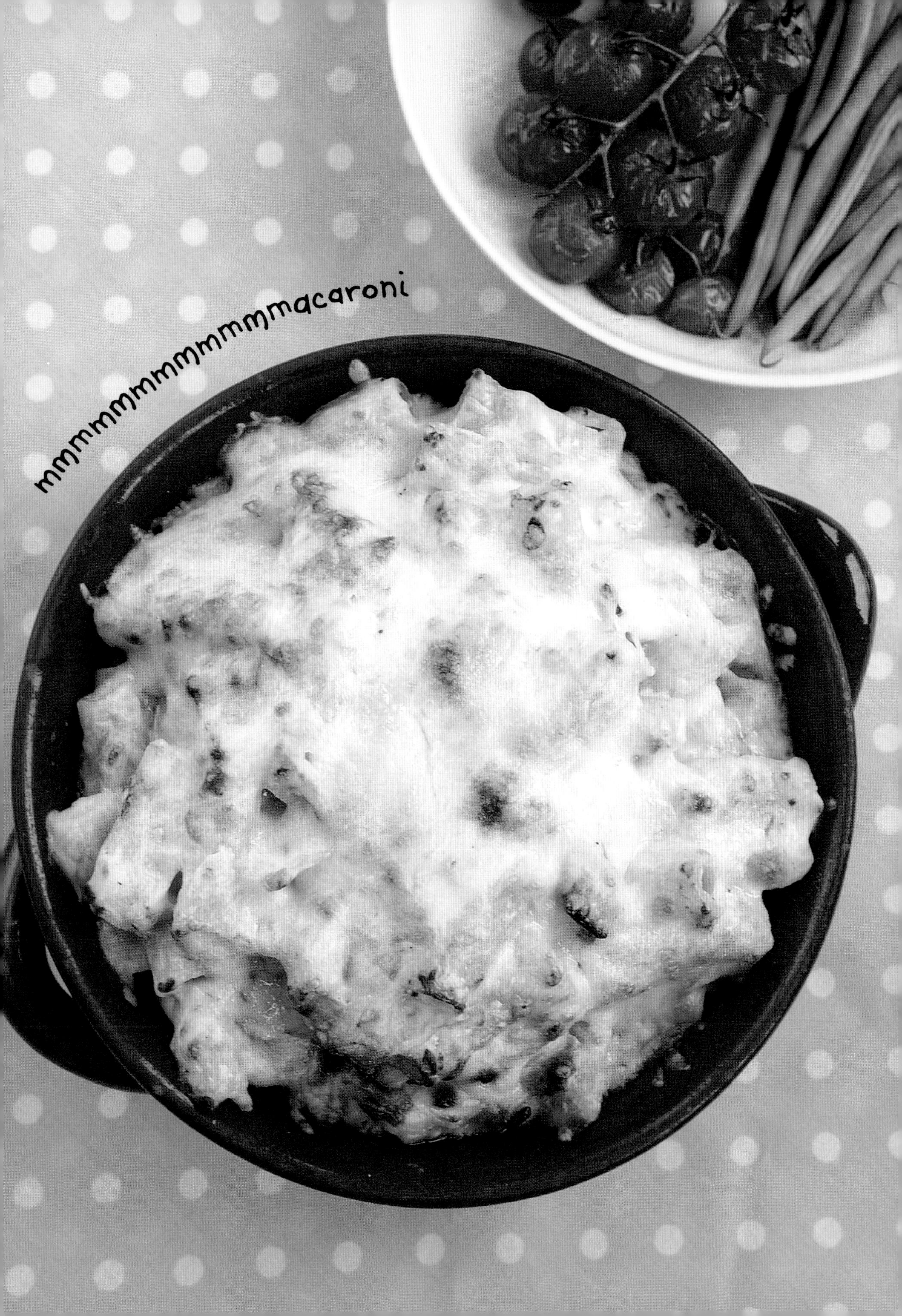
mmmmmmmmmmmmacaroni

How do fruit + veggies grow?

Picking food out of the ground or off a tree helps children to get a real sense of what food looks like before it arrives in the stores. Digging up potatoes makes for muddy fun; picking strawberries can turn fingers bright red. Scour your local paper and check online to see what pick-your-own possibilities there are near you.

① Go prepared

Make a date for the whole family to go together. Take gloves, disposable wipes, boots, and even a change of clothes—things could get grubby! Some pick-your-own farms have family centers where children can learn about the produce or see some animals.

What to choose?

Think about what works well for you all. Little ones will love picking strawberries, raspberries, and peas, which grow low to the ground. Older children may like reaching for apples or pears from big trees in an orchard.

② Pick + talk

While you pick, talk about everything you can feel, see, and smell. What does the soil feel like? What about the leaves? Are the fruit or veggies you're picking hard or soft? How are they different from what you buy in the stores? Do they have a different smell? Perhaps they even look different. Talk about big and small. For potatoes, onions, and large fruit, count them as you put them in the basket.

Go to market

If you can't get picking, visit a farmers' market, where the produce is fresh, fresh, fresh!

Heads up!

After apple or potato picking, try making your own fruit and veggie heads. Cut out two eyes, a nose, and a mouth from a magazine and stick them on. Add some yarn for hair or feathers to give feathery locks. Pom-poms with gem stickers make gorgeous ears complete with earrings!

③ At home

Wash your bounty together—who can scrub their potatoes cleanest? Taste the fruits as soon as you have washed them—deee-licious! Talk about your favorite ways to eat your hoard—then serve some of it for dinner. Yum!

Mmmmoussaka

serves **4** | prep **10** minutes | cook **50** minutes

Named after the sound little ones make when they eat it, this delicious dinner combines ground lamb with smooth sweet potato for a yummy twist. Using crème fraîche instead of a white sauce saves you time without losing any creaminess.

What you need

2–3 tablespoons **olive oil**

½ **onion**, chopped (optional)

8 ounces **lean ground lamb**

½ cup mashed **sweet potato**

1 small **eggplant**, sliced into circles about ½-inch thick

1 large **red-skinned** or **white round potato**, sliced

1 cup grated **cheddar cheese**

⅔ cup **crème fraîche**, **Greek yogurt**, or **white sauce**

Blow!

What to do

1. Preheat the oven to 400°F.

2. Heat 1 tablespoon of the oil in a saucepan, add the onion (if using), and cook for 3 minutes over medium heat, until softened. Add the meat and cook for 4–5 minutes. Then, reduce the heat, add the mashed sweet potato, and cook for another 1 minute. Remove from the heat; set aside.

3. Add the remaining oil to a large skillet and gently sauté the eggplant circles for 10 minutes, until soft.

4. Meanwhile, place the slices of potato in a large saucepan of water, bring to a boil, then reduce the heat to low and simmer uncovered for 10 minutes, until the potatoes are slightly softened but not mushy.

5. In a shallow ovenproof dish, put a layer of meat mixture followed by a layer of both potato and eggplant. Repeat with the remaining ingredients, finishing with a neat layer of the potato and eggplant slices.

6. In a bowl mix three-quarters of the grated cheese with the crème fraîche. Spread this mixture over the top layer of the moussaka. Sprinkle with the remaining cheese, then cook in the oven for about 30 minutes, until the top is golden and bubbling.

Ella's shortcut

To save having to mash up a sweet potato, try using 1 (4¼-ounce) pouch of Ella's Kitchen Sweet Potatoes, Pumpkin, Apples + Blueberries and you get the added benefit of fruity goodness, too!

Totally cool Caribbean chicken with mango + pineapple

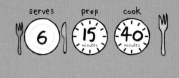

serves 6 | prep 15 minutes | cook 40 minutes

A flavor of the Caribbean makes this the most laid-back of dinners. Watch it bring happy, sunny smiles to everyone at your table.

What you need

1 tablespoon **sunflower oil**

3 skinless, boneless **chicken breasts** (about 1 pound), diced

1 **onion**, chopped

4 **Yukon gold** or **white round potatoes**, diced

1 **butternut squash**, diced

1 teaspoon **medium curry powder**

½ teaspoon **ground cumin**

¼ teaspoon **ground cinnamon**

A pinch of **turmeric**

1 cup **vegetable stock**

1 (14½-ounce) can **diced tomatoes**

1 **mango**, chopped into small pieces

1 (15-ounce) can **pineapple chunks** in natural juice, drained

What to do

1. Heat the oil in a large saucepan and cook the chicken and onion for 5 minutes, until the onion is soft. Add the potato, squash, and spices and cook for another 4–5 minutes, until the chicken is cooked through.

2. Add the vegetable stock and tomatoes to the pan and bring the sauce to a boil.

3. Stir in the chopped mango and the pineapple chunks, then reduce the heat to low, cover, and simmer for 20 minutes, stirring occasionally. Remove the lid and cook for another 10 minutes, until the liquid has reduced to a thick sauce.

4. Serve immediately with rice.

Freeze!

This makes a great dish for freezing so you can enjoy quick-fix Caribbean sunshine whatever the weather.

74

Zingy lamb + couscous with mangoes + raisins

Packed full of flavorsome fruit and veg, this couscous dish really does zing!

serves **6** · prep **15** minutes · cook **1¾** hours

omit green beans

What you need

2 tablespoons **olive oil**

1 **garlic** clove, crushed

12 ounces boneless **leg of lamb** or **lamb cutlets**, diced

1 **onion**, chopped

2 teaspoons **ground cumin**

½ teaspoon **ground cinnamon**

1 **carrot**, diced

2½ cups diced **butternut squash**

1 (14½-ounce) can **diced tomatoes**

2 cups **vegetable stock**

1 ripe **mango**, chopped into small pieces

1 cup ½-inch **green bean** pieces

1 cup **couscous**

⅔ cup **raisins**

What to do

1. Preheat the oven to 350°F.

2. Heat the oil in a skillet and sauté the garlic, lamb, onion, and spices for 5 minutes, until the lamb has browned on all sides. Transfer the mixture to a casserole dish.

3. Put the carrot and squash in the skillet and cook for 3–4 minutes, until softened, then add the tomatoes and 1¼ cups of the stock and bring the mixture to a boil.

4. As soon as the tomato-and-stock mixture starts to boil, remove it from the heat and stir it into the lamb. Add the chopped mango, stir together, then cover and bake in the oven for 1½ hours, until the lamb is tender.

5. Once the lamb is ready, boil the green beans in the remaining stock for 2–3 minutes, until just tender. Remove the beans from the liquid with a slotted spoon and set aside. Pour the stock into a liquid measuring cup and set aside.

6. Put the couscous and raisins into a heatproof bowl and add the beans. Check how much stock you have in the measuring cup—you'll need 1 cup, so top up the liquid with some boiling water, if necessary. Pour the liquid over the couscous. Cover it with plastic wrap and let it stand for 5 minutes, until moist. Fluff the couscous with a fork and serve it with the lamb.

Beef + mashed potato casserole

serves **6** prep **20** minutes cook **1** hour

omit peas

Hearty, comfort food—even if it's summer time—this is always a favorite with little and big ones alike.

What you need

5 **russet** or **Yukon gold potatoes**, diced

¼ cup **whole milk**

1½ cups diced **sweet potato**

1 **carrot**, diced

1 **onion**, chopped

1 pound **ground round** or **ground sirloin beef**

½ teaspoon **ground cinnamon**

1 cup **vegetable stock**

2 **tomatoes**, chopped

⅔ cup **frozen peas**, thawed

What to do

1. Preheat the oven to 400°F.

2. Cook the potatoes in boiling water for 10–15 minutes or until tender. Drain them and return them to the saucepan. Pour in the milk, then mash the potatoes well.

3. While the potatoes are cooking, in another saucepan, cook the sweet potato and carrot in boiling water for 10 minutes. Drain them and coarsely mash.

4. Cook the onion, ground beef, and cinnamon in a large saucepan for 5 minutes, until the meat is completely brown. Add the stock, the mashed sweet potato–and–carrot mixture, and the tomatoes to the meat and cook for 5 minutes. Add the peas, give it a stir, and transfer it all to an ovenproof serving dish. Top with the mashed potatoes and bake in the oven for 30 minutes, until golden.

Ella's shortcut

To save on some chopping time, replace the sweet potato and carrots with 1 (4¼-ounce) pouch of Ella's Kitchen Spinach, Apples + Rutabagas and reduce the amount of stock to 1 cup.

79

Squashy salmon fish cakes

serves **2+2** adults + kids

prep **20** minutes + cooling

cook **25** minutes

omit green beans

Break out your artistic side and create loads of squashy fishy goodness
with plenty of splashy fishy style.

What you need

4 **russet** or **Yukon gold potatoes**, cut into large dice

1 **carrot**, cut into small dice

8 ounces **salmon fillets**, skin removed

3 tablespoons **sunflower oil**

1 small **leek**, thinly sliced

¼ cup finely chopped **green bean** pieces

2 tablespoons finely chopped **flat-leaf parsley**

Blowing bubbles

Turn the plate into a work of art—ask your little one to arrange a few peas as if the fishy fish cakes were blowing bubbles.

What to do

1. Cook the potatoes and carrot in boiling water for 15 minutes, until tender. Drain and mash them together, and set the mash aside to cool.

2. Meanwhile, poach the salmon in simmering water for 5 minutes, until cooked through, then let cool. Break up the fish into flakes, being careful to make sure that there are no bones.

3. Heat 1 tablespoon of the oil in a large skillet and cook the leek and beans for 5 minutes, until tender. Stir them into the mashed carrot-and-potatoes, then add the cooked salmon and parsley to the mixture and stir again.

4. Using your hands, mold the mixture into 2 large fish cakes and 2 smaller fish cakes. (Fishy shapes look great.)

5. Heat the remaining oil in a skillet and cook the fish cakes for 5 minutes, turning once, until golden on both sides and warm through. Serve immediately with some peas.

Color us in

Punchy pork + apple casserole

serves 6 · prep 15 minutes · cook 2¼ hours

omit green beans

Pork and apples always make a great combination and this full-of-flavor dish is no exception. It's perfect for a warming dinner.

What you need

2 tablespoons **sunflower oil**

1 pound **pork loin**, diced

5 **red-skinned** or **white round potatoes**, thinly sliced

1 **onion**, sliced

2 **carrots**, sliced

1 **leek**, sliced

1 **garlic** clove, crushed

1 teaspoon **dried mixed herbs**

½ cup halved **green beans**

1 **Pippin apple** (or other sweet, crisp apple), cored and sliced

1¼ cups **vegetable stock**

What to do

1. Preheat the oven to 350°F.

2. Heat 1 tablespoon of the oil in a skillet, add the pork, and cook for about 5 minutes, turning occasionally until the meat has browned on all sides.

3. Meanwhile, use half of the sliced potatoes to make a thin potato layer in the bottom of a casserole dish. Spoon the browned pork on top.

4. In the same skillet, heat the remaining 1 tablespoon of oil and sauté the onion, carrots, leek, garlic, and herbs for 5 minutes, until the onion, leek, and garlic are soft.

5. Spoon the vegetables over the top of the pork and then sprinkle with the beans. Top with a layer of sliced apple and finally the remaining sliced potatoes. Pour the vegetable stock over the top. Cover the casserole and bake in the oven for 1¾ hours. Remove the lid and continue to bake for another 15 minutes, or until the potatoes are golden.

Layer patterns

Can I help?

Ask your little helpers to make the layers of potato and apple in the casserole—can they make a pattern with the slices?

Ella's shortcut

If you want to save some time, replace the apple slices with 1 (2½-ounce) pouch of Ella's Kitchen Apples, Apples, Apples. Stir it into the vegetable mixture.

Oink

Wonderfully warming fruity beef stew

serves **6** · prep **25** minutes · cook **2¼** hours

This is another of Ella's favorite meals—from her mom. Adding preserves to the stew gives it a really fruity, tasty punch.

What you need

2 tablespoons **olive oil**

1¾ pounds boneless **beef chuck** or **round**, diced

1 **onion**, thinly sliced

5 **carrots**, sliced

2 **plums** or **apricots**, pitted and sliced

1 **garlic** clove, crushed

1 tablespoon **tomato paste**

2 tablespoons **all-purpose flour**

Finely grated rind of 1 **lemon**, plus 1 tablespoon of the juice

3 cups **beef stock**

½ cup **plum** or **damson preserves**

Freshly ground **black pepper**

What to do

1. Preheat the oven to 315°F.

2. Heat the oil in a large casserole dish. Add the beef, in batches, and cook for 3–4 minutes, until browned on all sides. Remove each batch with a slotted spoon and set aside.

3. Add the onion to the casserole and cook for 2 minutes, until softened. Add the carrots, plums or apricots, garlic, tomato paste, and flour and cook for another 2 minutes.

4. Return the browned beef and all its juices to the casserole along with the lemon rind and juice, beef stock, and preserves. Season with the black pepper and bring to a simmer.

5. Cover and cook in the oven for 2 hours, until the beef is tender. Serve with pasta or mashed potatoes.

Spoon skills

Can I help?

Even very little ones like to show their skills with a spoon or fork. Ask your toddler to give you a hand spooning in the preserves at the end of the method. If they get sticky fingers? All the better to lick!

Fun salmon + veggie packages

makes **4** parcels prep **10** minutes cook **30** minutes

This is a great way to cook simple, fresh ingredients. Wrapping the ingredients in shiny foil packages makes them seem extra special.

What you need

Olive oil, for drizzling

10 **new potatoes**, thickly sliced, skin on

1½ cups **broccoli florets**

1 **red bell pepper**, cut into thick strips

6 **baby corn**, halved lengthwise

½ teaspoon **dried mixed herbs**

2 tablespoons **tomato paste**

4 **salmon fillets**, skin removed

What to do

1. Preheat the oven to 400°F.

2. Drizzle four large squares of aluminum foil with a little olive oil and make a small pile of the vegetable ingredients in the center of each. Sprinkle each pile with some herbs.

3. Spread ½ tablespoon of the tomato paste over each of the salmon fillets. Place 1 fillet on top of each pile of vegetables. Scrunch up the foil pieces, leaving a small gap in the top of each package to let the steam escape. Place the packages on a baking sheet and bake in the oven for 30 minutes, until the vegetables are tender and the salmon is cooked through.

Go pesto!

Pesto (try our Green Pasta Sauce on page 96) makes a delicious alternative to the tomato paste.

Foil scrunch-up

Can I help?

Your children will love helping you construct the packages—especially when it comes to scrunching up that noisy foil. Marvel together at how the contents have miraculously transformed when the packages come out of the oven.

Five ways with potatoes

Who knew potatoes could be so tasty? Gone are the days of bland mashed potatoes. Encourage little ones to make shapes from the potato peelings—or see who can peel the longest strip (under supervision, of course).

Rosemary roasties

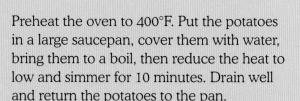

serves **6** — prep **10** minutes — cook **1** hour

6 **russet potatoes** or 1½ pounds **new potatoes**, cut into chunks

3 tablespoons **sunflower oil**

1 tablespoon **rosemary** leaves

Preheat the oven to 400°F. Put the potatoes in a large saucepan, cover them with water, bring them to a boil, then reduce the heat to low and simmer for 10 minutes. Drain well and return the potatoes to the pan.

Add the oil and shake the pan a little to coat the potato cubes. Transfer them to a baking sheet, drizzle with any excess oil left in the pan, and sprinkle with the rosemary. Bake in the oven for 45–55 minutes, until golden and crispy, turning the chunks after 30 minutes to make sure they go crispy all over.

Herbed mash up

serves **6** — prep **10** minutes — cook **15** minutes

6 **Yukon gold** or **russet potatoes**, cut into chunks

2 tablespoons **unsalted butter**

2 **garlic** cloves, crushed

¼ cup **whole milk**

2 tablespoons finely chopped **flat-leaf parsley**, or 2 tablespoons chopped **chives** and ¼ cup **crème fraîche** or **sour cream** (optional)

Put the potatoes in a large saucepan, cover them with water, bring them to a boil, then reduce the heat to low and simmer for 10–15 minutes, until tender, then drain.

Put the empty pan back on the heat. Melt the butter and add the garlic, then sauté for 1 minute, until soft. Remove the pan from the heat. Add the potatoes and milk and mash well, then stir in the parsley.

Alternatively, mash the potatoes with the milk and stir in the crème fraîche or sour cream and chopped chives in place of the parsley.

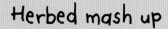

Baby baked potatoes

serves 6 | prep 2 minutes | cook 45 minutes

1 lb 9 ounces **new potatoes**

1 tablespoon **olive oil**

Preheat the oven to 400°F.

Place the potatoes on a baking sheet and sprinkle over the oil. Toss to coat evenly. Bake for 45 minutes or until golden and cooked all the way through.

Sweet potato fishy fries

serves 6 | prep 5 minutes | cook 30 minutes

4 **sweet potatoes**, cut into thick slices

1 tablespoon **sunflower oil**

2 tablespoons **maple syrup**

Preheat the oven to 400°F. Use a fish-shaped cutter to cut your sweet potato slices into fish-shaped fries. Put them in a large roasting pan, add the oil and maple syrup, and toss to coat. Spread the fries out on a baking sheet and bake for 25–30 minutes, until tender, turning once.

Cheesy fries

serves 6 | prep 2 minutes | cook 25 minutes

1½ pounds frozen **oven chips**

¾ cup grated **cheddar cheese**

Preheat the oven to 425°F. Spread the fries out on a large baking sheet and cook for 20–25 minutes or according to the package directions, until golden. Sprinkle with the cheese. Toss well until the cheese has melted slightly, then return to the oven for 1 minute.

Teeny-weeny turkey burger bites

makes **6** | prep **35** minutes + proving | cook **20** minutes

These teeny-weeny turkey burgers are beautifully lean and just right for little hands to hold. If you can't find ground turkey, ground chicken will work just as well. We made our own rolls using pizza-crust mix, but use store-bought mini-hamburger rolls if you're short of time.

What you need

6 ounces **lean ground turkey**

¾ cup fresh **white bread crumbs**

2 **egg yolks**

A large pinch of **dried mixed herbs** or 2 teaspoons finely chopped fresh **oregano**

A splash of **Worcestershire sauce** (optional)

Freshly ground **black pepper** (optional)

2 teaspoons **vegetable oil**

Slices of **tomato** and **cucumber**, to serve (optional)

For the rolls

1 (6½-ounce) box **pizza-crust mix**

1 **egg**, beaten

Sesame seeds, for sprinkling

What to do

1. Preheat the oven to 425°F. To make your mini rolls, make the pizza dough according to the package directions. Mold the dough into six ping-pong ball-size rolls. Cover with a damp cloth and let rise for 30 minutes, or until they have doubled in size. Place the rolls on a baking sheet and put them in the oven for 10 minutes, until they sound hollow when you tap the bottom. Remove them from the oven, brush them with the beaten egg, sprinkle with the sesame seeds, and return to the oven for 2–3 minutes, until they are golden on top.

2. While the rolls are cooking, make the burgers. Mix together the ground meat, bread crumbs, egg yolk, herbs, and Worcestershire sauce (if using) in a bowl with a little freshly ground black pepper (if using), until the mixture is fully combined and moist but holds together.

3. Divide the mixture into six equal portions, then flour your hands and roll each portion into a ball and gently flatten it into a patty.

4. Brush a nonstick skillet with the oil, then put it over low–medium heat and cook the burgers for 8–10 minutes, turning once, until they are completely cooked through.

5. Serve immediately in a mini-burger roll with a couple of slices of cucumber and a slice of tomato (if using).

Bite me

Quick quesadillas

serves 2 | prep 10 minutes | cook 20 minutes

Eat like a Mexican. We think these delicious quesadillas provide a perfect opportunity for a fiesta atmosphere—how about giving out some moustaches and party whistles?

What you need

1 tablespoon **olive oil**

1 skinless, bonless **chicken breast** (about 5 ounces), sliced into strips

½ **red bell pepper**, cut into strips

2 teaspoons **balsamic vinegar**

2 **flour tortillas**

1 tablespoon chopped **cilantro**

½ cup grated **Swiss**, **cheddar**, or **American cheese**

What to do

1. Heat the oil in a skillet and cook the chicken and bell pepper for 3–4 minutes, adding the balsamic vinegar for the final 1 minute of cooking, until the chicken is cooked through and the bell pepper is soft.

2. In a separate skillet, lay a flour tortilla in the bottom of the skillet and top with the cooked chicken and bell pepper and the cilantro. Sprinkle with the cheese and top with the other tortilla.

3. Cover the skillet with a lid and cook over a gentle heat for 12 minutes, or until the bottom of the tortilla is golden. Flip the tortilla over in the skillet (you'll need two spatulas for this), and cook it for another 1–2 minutes, until the bottom is golden and the cheese has melted. Remove the tortilla from the skillet and slice it into wedges.

4. Let cool slightly before serving.

Slurp me

Marvelous meatballs

makes **24** · prep **10** minutes · cook **20** minutes

This basic mixture will make handfuls of meatballs that are ideal for play-date dinners. We've served them here with our Great Tomato Sauce, but they're delicious inside our Pizza Pocket Bites (see page 153), too.

What you need

3 tablespoons **apple puree** or **applesauce**

¼ cup fresh **bread crumbs**

2 tablespoons finely chopped **sage** leaves

1 pound **lean ground pork**

½ teaspoon **ground nutmeg**

1 tablespoon **vegetable oil**

What to do

1. To make the apple puree, peel, core, and chop two sweet, crisp apples. Steam until soft, then mash with a fork. (Freeze any leftovers.)

2. Place the bread crumbs and sage in a large bowl and add ¼ cup of boiling water. Let the mixture soak for 2–3 minutes, until the water has been absorbed and the mixture is cool enough to handle.

3. Add the pork, apple puree, and nutmeg and use your hands to mix together the ingredients until fully combined and stiff. Mold the mixture into 24 mini meatballs.

4. Heat the oil in a large skillet and cook the meatballs over low heat for 15 minutes, turning occasionally, until cooked through. (You may need to do this in batches, in which case set each batch aside on a warm plate.)

5. Serve the meatballs on a mound of spaghetti topped with plenty of our Great Tomato Sauce (see page 32).

Freeze!

If you aren't using all the meatballs at once, you can freeze them (uncooked, or cooked and then cooled completely) for up to a month.

Ella's shortcut

If you don't want to spend time making the apple puree, you can substitute the same amount of Ella's Kitchen Apples, Apples, Apples instead.

Three easy pasta sauces

We asked kids what their favorite pasta sauces were. Red, green, and white were the most popular replies! Whatever your child's favorite, these thee sauces are packed full of good tasty stuff and work stirred into any shape, size, or color of pasta.

Red pasta sauce

serves **6** prep **5** minutes cook **17** minutes

- 1 tablespoon **sunflower oil**
- 1 **onion**, chopped
- 8 ounces **unsmoked bacon**, chopped
- 2 teaspoons **paprika**
- 6 **tomatoes**, coarsely chopped
- 2/3 cup **vegetable stock**
- 2 tablespoons finely chopped **flat-leaf parsley**

1. Heat the oil in a large saucepan and sauté the onion and bacon for 4–5 minutes. Add the paprika and tomatoes and cook for 5 minutes.

2. Add the vegetable stock to the tomatoes, and simmer, uncovered, for 5–7 minutes. Stir in the parsley.

Green pasta sauce

serves **6** prep **5** minutes cook **3** minutes

- 1/3 cup **extra-virgin olive oil**
- 2 **garlic** cloves, coarsely chopped
- 3/4 cup **pine nuts**
- 2 cups **basil**
- 1/2 cup freshly grated **Parmesan cheese**

1. Heat 1 tablespoon of the oil in a small skillet and sauté the garlic and pine nuts for 2–3 minutes, until they turn golden.

2. Place the basil in a food processor and process to coarsely chop, add the pine nut mixture, remaining oil, Parmesan and 1/2 cup of water. Process to create a coarse paste.

White pasta sauce

serves **6** prep **5** minutes cook **6** minutes

- 2 tablespoons **unsalted butter**
- 1/3 cup **all-purpose flour**
- 2 cups **whole milk**
- 1 cup **green bean** pieces
- 2 (5-ounce) cans **tuna in spring water**, drained
- 1/2 cup **pitted black olives**, sliced
- 1/2 cup grated **cheddar cheese**
- 1 tablespoon finely chopped **chives**

1. Melt the butter in a saucepan and stir in the flour. Cook for 1 minute, then gradually add the milk. Add the green beans and bring to a boil, stirring until thickened. Simmer for 3–4 minutes, or until the green beans are tender.

2. Stir in the tuna, olives, and cheese and cook for 1 minute to melt the cheese. Stir in the chives.

Lovely lasagne

serves 6 | prep 20 minutes | cook 50 minutes

So many moms tell us that they avoid making lasagne because it takes so long to prepare. This version (and its veggie alternative) will take you only 20 minutes—just plain easy. Why not cook up a big batch and freeze it in portions?

What you need

1 **onion**, chopped

1 pound **ground round** or **ground sirloin beef**

1 **carrot**, diced

3 cups sliced **mushrooms**

1 teaspoon **dried mixed herbs**

½ teaspoon grated **nutmeg**

1 (14½-ounce) can **diced tomatoes**

6 dried **lasagna noodles**

1 **egg**, beaten

1 cup **crème fraîche** or **Greek yogurt**

½ cup grated **cheddar cheese**

What to do

1. Preheat the oven to 400°F.

2. Sauté the onion, ground beef, and carrot in a large saucepan for 2–3 minutes, until the meat is brown. Stir in the mushrooms, herbs, nutmeg, tomatoes, and ⅔ cup water. Bring the sauce to a boil, then reduce the heat to low and simmer, covered, for 10 minutes, stirring occasionally.

3. Meanwhile, cook the lasagna noodles in boiling water for 5–6 minutes, drain, then cool.

4. Mix the egg with the crème fraîche or yogurt.

5. Place one-third of the meat mixture in the bottom of a shallow ovenproof dish, then make a layer with two lasagna noodles and spoon over another third of the meat. Top with another two lasagna noodles and then the remaining of the meat mixture. Layer with the remaining noodles and pour the crème fraîche-and-egg mixture over the top. Finally, sprinkle with the cheese and bake in the oven for 30–35 minutes, until the top is golden.

6. Serve warm with a salad.

Go veggie

For a vegetarian option, sauté the onion and carrot as in the meat version, then add 1 diced eggplant, 1 diced zucchini, and ¾ cup vegetable stock. Add the mushrooms, herbs, nutmeg, and tomatoes, cover the pan, and simmer for 10 minutes, stirring occasionally. Continue as for the meat recipe from step 3 onward.

Can I help?

Layer it up

Parboiled lasagna noodles should be fairly robust for little hands to handle, so ask your toddler to help you make the pasta layers; you do the meat and he or she does the noodles. This way lasagne making is a team effort!

Cool kiddie café

Today's specials

Children love to play at being grown-ups and what better way than to set up their own outdoor café in the yard. This is a great play-date activity, or a wonderful way to involve the whole family in playing together. Of course, you can move the café inside on rainy days.

Make a menu

★ menu ★

Get creative with your menu. Find some paper, pens, stickers, glue, and cutouts of food photos from magazines and create a mouthwatering list of items that are on sale at your café. Don't forget the tea, coffee, and juices, too. If you have a wipe-clean drawing board or blackboard, you can create a specials list—let your little ones set the prices.

Pretend pizza

Try making pretend pizza slices out of cardboard—use differently colored tissue paper for the toppings and cotton balls as melty cheese. If your customers demand pasta—no problem! Use yellow yarn to make a bowl of delicious noodles.

2

Lay the table

Find a brightly colored blanket or sheet to use as a tablecloth. If you don't have an outdoor table, make this a picnic café and lay your tablecloth on the ground, using cushions for seats. Are there any flowers you could pick in the yard to put in a little cup in the middle of the table? Give them a sniff— do they smell beautiful? Don't forget the plastic knives and forks and some tea-set cups and saucers.

3

Gather your food

Use playdough to make cakes or pretend sandwiches for your café; while grass from the yard can make a pretend salad. You could also use real fruit, as well as water for tea and coffee.

4

Play your roles

Decide which of you will be the waiters, who will be the customers, and who will pretend to be the chef. Find aprons for the waiters and chef (who might need a hat, too, if you have one) and don't forget pen and paper to take orders. Show your customers to their seats and hand them their menus. What do the customers think of the food?

Afternoon treat

When the game is over, keep the outdoor café and serve a real snack there for your little ones. They will love it when you are the waiter or waitress serving real food in their café—will they leave you a tip?

Full-of-Sunshine Thai curry

Bursting with bright colors, this gentle introduction to Thai flavors provides plenty of adventure for tiny taste buds.

What you need

1 tablespoon **vegetable oil**

½ **butternut squash**, peeled, seeded, and diced

1 large **onion**, diced

1 **carrot**, sliced

1 **red bell pepper**, sliced

1½ cups **sugar snap peas**

1¼-inch piece fresh **ginger**, grated

1 **garlic** clove, crushed

1 teaspoon **ground cumin**

½ teaspoon **mild chili powder**

1¾ cups canned **coconut milk**

1 **vegetable bouillon cube**, crumbled

A large handful of **cilantro**, finely chopped

4 **lime** wedges, to serve (optional)

What to do

1. Heat the oil in a large skillet and cook the squash, onion, and carrot for 5 minutes unil the onion is soft. Add the bell pepper, sugar snap peas, ginger, garlic, and spices and sauté for 2–3 minutes, stirring occasionally.

2. Stir in the coconut milk and crumbled bouillon cube, cover, and simmer for 10 minutes, stirring occasionally, until the vegetables are tender. Stir in the cilantro.

3. Serve the curry with long-grain rice and lime wedges (if using).

Thai-taste-tastic!

Thai food is famously fragrant, which makes this a fabulous meal for encouraging your toddler to explore how smell and taste work together. Offer the cut ginger root and a few cilantro leaves for a sniff fest. Talk about the different smells. Can your toddler taste those smells when he or she digs into the bowl of cooked curry?

Chick-chick chicken pasta casserole

serves 6 | prep 15 minutes | cook 45 minutes

Inspired by the Dale family—mom and dad work at Ella's making sure all our food is safe to eat—this comforting pasta dish is easy to make and topped with cheesy bread crumbs.

What you need

½ **butternut squash**, peeled, seeded, and diced

1 **carrot**, diced

1 teaspoon **olive oil**

1 skinless, boneless **chicken breast** (about 5 ounces), diced

1½ cups finely sliced **mushrooms**

⅓ cup **whole milk**

4 ounces small **pasta** shapes, such as pasta shells

1 thick slice of **country-style bread**

¼ cup grated **cheddar cheese**

Ella's shortcut

If you don't want to puree the squash for this recipe, you can substitute it with 1 (4¼-ounce) pouch of Ella's Kitchen Butternut Squash, Carrots, Apples + Prunes instead.

What to do

1. Preheat the oven to 400°F.

2. Steam the butternut squash and carrot pieces for 10 minutes, until tender, then process them together with a handheld immersion blender until you have a soft puree.

3. Heat the oil in a medium saucepan and add the chicken pieces. Cook the chicken for 10 minutes, turning occasionally, until cooked through, then add the mushrooms and cook for another 4–5 minutes. Stir in ½ cup of the butternut squash-and-carrot puree (freeze any leftovers), then add the milk, stir, and cook for another 1 minute. Remove the mixture from the heat.

4. Meanwhile, cook the pasta according to the package directions until al dente. Drain, then add the pasta to the chicken mixture and mix together thoroughly. Transfer everything to a small, shallow ovenproof dish.

5. Using a food processor, process the bread into bread crumbs, then place them in abowl and stir through the grated cheddar. Spoon the cheesy bread crumb mixture over the pasta casserole and cook in the oven for 20 minutes, until the top is golden brown and crispy.

Perfect Desserts

Have you tried
the Swirly Whirly
Cheesecake?
It's my favorite!

Love, Ella x

Baby baked apples

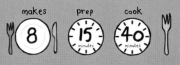

When these come out of the oven, a gooey, sticky sauce will have appeared as if by magic.

What you need

8 small sweet, crisp **apples**

4 tablepsoons **unsalted butter**

¼ cup packed **brown sugar**

1 teaspoon **ground cinnamon**

⅓ cup **raisins**

Juice of ½ **orange**

Squeeeeezy juicy

Whether you have a citrus press or a hand citrus juicer, pressing down on the flesh of the orange and watching the delicious juice come out is pure culinary magic for little ones. Put the juice in a measuring cup to see how much you managed to squeeze out.

What to do

1. Preheat the oven to 350°F. Wash and dry the apples. Cut a triangular-shape cavity from each, removing most of the core at the same time, but keeping the bottom of the apple intact. Place the apples in a baking dish.

2. Mix together the butter and sugar, then stir in the cinnamon and raisins. Fill each of the apples with the cinnamon-and-raisin butter, then drizzle them with orange juice.

3. Place the apples in a baking dish and bake them for 40 minutes, until soft and beginning to turn golden. Serve with spoonfuls of crème fraîche or Greek yogurt.

What shapes can you make?

Toasty, fruity brioche

Orange-colored fruit, such as peaches, mangoes, and apricots—fresh or canned—work best for this delicious dessert. Serve it plain or with Greek yogurt or crème fraîche. If you prefer, you can swap the brioche for croissants.

What you need

6 slices **brioche**

2 tablespoons **unsalted butter**, softened

2 tablespoons **apricot preserves**

1 **mango**, 2 **nectarines**, 2 **peaches**, 6 **apricots**, or a mixture of any, pitted and sliced

1 tablespoon packed **brown sugar**

¼ cup freshly squeezed **orange juice**

What to do

1. Preheat the oven to 400°F. Butter each slice of brioche, then place the slices into a baking dish so that they fit snugly together and spread them with the apricot preserves.

2. Place the sliced fruit on top of the brioche until the brioche is completely covered and you have used all the fruit.

3. Sprinkle over the sugar and drizzle with the orange juice so that the brioche is moist.

4. Bake the dessert in the oven for 20 minutes, until the brioche is slightly crisped and browned at the edges. Serve hot.

Fruity fun

Can I help?

In creating this recipe, the children can have all the creative fun—putting the fruit on top of the brioche slices and making a pattern on top. Lay out the slices of fruit for them, step back, and watch them have fun.

Color me in

111

Big banana + honey dream

A match made in heaven, banana and honey make a dreamy combination that wraps a warm hug around the taste buds.

What you need

- ⅔ cup **heavy cream**
- 3 ripe **bananas**
- 1 cup **Greek yogurt**
- 2 tablespoons **honey**
- 1 tablespoon **lemon juice**
- **Chocolate disks** or other shapes, or juicy **mango** slices, to decorate

What to do

1. Whip the cream until soft peaks form. Mash the bananas on a plate and then transfer them to a bowl.

2. Stir the yogurt, honey, and lemon juice into the banana, then gently fold in the whipped cream.

3. Spoon the mixture into six individual serving dishes and decorate with the chocolate disks or mango slices.

Causing a stir

Can I help?

Tiny tots will love having a turn at whipping the cream and stirring the mixture all together. With chocolate shapes or mango, the results are always irresistible.

112

Perfect pear + raspberry oaty crisp

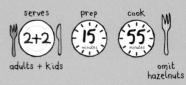

serves 2+2 adults + kids | prep 15 minutes | cook 55 minutes omit hazelnuts

Making a crisp is so much fun for little hands, and pears and raspberries are among the most perfect sweet partners for a fruity crisp. This delicious dessert definitely deserves to round off a family Sunday roast.

What you need

¼ cup **sugar**

3 **large pears**, or 1 (15-ounce) **can pears**, drained

1 cup **raspberries**

For the crumb topping

2 cups **all-purpose flour**

1 stick **unsalted butter**

½ cup firmly packed **light brown sugar**

½ cup **rolled oats**

½ cup chopped **hazelnuts** (optional)

What to do

1. Preheat the oven to 350°F.

2. If you're using fresh pears, put the sugar into a large saucepan with 4 cups of water. Place the pears in the pan. Bring up to a simmer and poach the pears for 20 minutes, until cooked through and tender. Drain them and let sit until they are cool enough to handle, then cut in half and remove the cores.

3. Slice the poached pears lengthwise. Place them in a 1-quart ovenproof dish. If you're using canned pears, coarsely chop them and put them into the dish. Add the raspberries and toss everything together.

4. To make the topping, put the flour into a bowl and add the butter. Rub the butter into the flour with your fingertips until it resembles bread crumbs. Stir in the sugar and rolled oats along with the hazelnuts (if using).

5. Spread the crumb mixture onto a baking sheet and place it in the oven for 10 minutes. This will give you a beautiful crunchy crumb topping. Remove it from the oven and sprinkle it over the fruit. Cook the crisp for 25 minutes, until golden. Serve warm with vanilla ice cream, crème fraîche, or whipped cream

Can I help?

Crumbly fingers

Encourage your toddler to rub the crumb mixture gently between his or her fingertips—see if they can make it look like rain as it is sprinkled into the bowl.

Pour me over

Eat me before I melt

The melty one

serves 8 | prep 10 minutes | cook 4–5 minutes

This healthy variation on a traditional baked Alaska uses frozen yogurt instead of ice cream. Dig in quickly to experience the hot and cold sensation.

What you need

3 **egg whites**

⅓ cup **superfine sugar**

¼ teaspoon **cream of tartar**

2–3 scoops **frozen fruit yogurt** (strawberry or raspberry works best)

1 store-bought **plain pound cake**, cut in half (or make your own, see below)

Make your cake

If you have time, why not make your own pound cake? Preheat the oven to 315°F. Cream together 1½ sticks unsalted butter and ¾ cup granulated sugar in a bowl, then beat in 3 lightly beaten extra-large eggs a little at a time. Sift in 2 cups all-purpose flour with 2 teaspoons baking powder and fold it in, followed by the juice and finely grated rind of a lemon. Put the batter into a parchment-lined 9 x 5 x 3-inch loaf pan and bake in the middle of the oven for about 40–50 minutes, until golden brown on top and a tootpick inserted in the center comes out clean.

What to do

1. Preheat the oven to 425°F.

2. Place the egg whites in a medium bowl and beat them until the mixture forms peaks. Add the cream of tartar and beat again for another 1 minute.

3. Add the sugar a little at a time, beating well after each addition, to make a meringue.

4. Place the cake on a baking sheet, with the two halves next to each other.

5. Place the scoops of frozen yogurt on top of the cake, leaving a 1¼-inch rim around the yogurt.

6. Coat the entire cake and frozen yogurt in the meringue, being careful to leave no gaps.

7. Bake the dessert in the oven for 4–5 minutes, until the meringue begins to turn golden.

8. Remove the baking sheet from the oven and serve the dessert immediately with a few pieces of fresh fruit to complement the yogurt flavor, if you like.

Playing stores

Creating your own store together is a perfect opportunity for play involving all five senses. A convenience store is a great way to start—and will fire your children's imaginations to think about the fruit and vegetables they so often see at mealtimes. Keep it varied by using different "goods" each time you play.

① Make your signs

Every store needs an open and closed sign. Grab some cardboard (the inside of a cereal box will do) and get creative. You can write the words, but let the little ones decorate.

Make a kiosk

Take a large cardboard box (big enough for a little face to appear in), then using a craft knife, cut a flap for the store window where goods and play cash change hands. Together, decorate the outside of the kiosk with lettering and stickers and make a sign that says "Pay here."

2

Choose your stock

It's time to raid the refrigerator! Borrow a few tomatoes, carrots, and onions, and any other vegetables that your toddler wants you to sell in the store—but nothing too perishable. Don't forget the fruit and herbs, too. Talk about the colors, smells, and textures.

Use some play money, or make some out of colored paper rectangles and cardboard circles. Don't forget to give change!

3

Make a display

Group together your chosen foods—will you put them together by color or by type? Count how many different kinds of food you have. Make the display look beautiful. You might, for example, set it out like a rainbow, or lay the foods out like a face, a train, or other shape. Decorate little labels to put next to each item. How much does everything cost?

4

Go shopping

You start off as the store owner and ask your toddler to visit with a favorite toy. Ask them to bring a shopping bag or basket. What would they like to buy today? Encourage them to "try before you buy"— so they even get to taste the products, too.

50 cents

$1.50

10 cents

Swirly whirly cheesecake

This is definitely among Ella's favorite desserts of all time—it's a delicious sweet treat without any added sugar. Enjoy it when you have friends to dinner.

What you need

- 1¾ ounces **roasted hazelnuts**, finely chopped
- 4 ounces **oatmeal cookies** or **graham crackers**, broken up
- ⅓ cup **pitted dates**
- 4 tablespoons **unsalted butter**, melted
- 1¾ cups **cream cheese**
- 1 teaspoon **vanilla extract**
- 2 cups hulled **strawberries**, pureed, plus extra to serve (optional)
- 1¼ cups **heavy cream**

What to do

1. Line the bottom of an 8-inch loose-bottom cake pan with parchment paper. Put the hazelnuts and cookies in a food processor and process them for a few seconds until everything is finely chopped and looks like bread crumbs. Add the dates and process again until the mixture is soft. Add the melted butter, mix well, and press the mixture into the pan with the back of a spoon. Chill it in the refrigerator for 15 minutes.

2. Meanwhile, make the topping. In a bowl, mix together the cream cheese, vanilla extract, and three-quarters of the pureed strawberries.

3. Whisk the cream until it is stiff, but still soft. Fold it gently into the cream cheese mixture. Remove the crust from the refrigerator and spoon the topping over it.

4. Drizzle with the remaining strawberry puree in an outward spiral from the center and then run a toothpick through the spiral to create a marbled effect. Chill the cheesecake in the refrigerator for at least 1 hour and then serve with strawberries on the side (if using).

Can I help?

Marble-ous!

Try out your tot's artistic talents by asking him or her to try making the swirly-whirly marbling pattern on the top of the cheesecake.

Ella's shortcut

You can sidestep making the strawberry puree by substituting 2 (3¼-ounce) pouches of Ella's Kitchen Smoothie Fruits—The Red One.

Strawberry mush up

This is a straightforward dessert to put together. Ripe juicy strawberries, cool creamy yogurt, and crunchy sweet meringue pieces create a festival of taste and texture. If you like, you can drizzle extra strawberry puree on top and decorate with a few extra berries.

What you need

4 store-bought **meringue** nests (or make your own, see below)

2 cups chopped, hulled **strawberries**, plus another 1 cup fresh hulled or frozen strawberries, pureed

1 cup **Greek yogurt**

Make your meringue

If you have time, try making your own meringues. Preheat the oven to 225°F. Whisk 3 egg whites until stiff, then whisk in ¾ cup superfine sugar, a teaspoon at a time. Whisk until the meringue is thick and glossy. Mix 1 teaspoon each of cornstarch and white wine vinegar with ½ teaspoon vanilla extract, and whisk this into the meringue. Spoon the mixture into 4 mounds on a parchment-lined baking sheet. Bake for 50–60 minutes.

What to do

1. Use your hands to break up the meringue nests into small pieces in a large mixing bowl. Add the chopped strawberries, reserving a few for decoration, and stir in the yogurt.

2. Add 2 tablespoons of pureed strawberries and stir through the yogurt gently to make the mixture streaky.

3. Spoon the mixture into six glasses or bowls, decorate with a few strawberry pieces, and add an extra drizzle of puree, if you like. Serve while the meringue is still crunchy.

Ella's shortcut

If you prefer, you can substitute the strawberry puree with 2 tablespoons of Ella's Kitchen Smoothie Fruits—The Red One.

Creamy coconut rice pudding with chunky mango sauce

serves 6–8   prep 20 minutes   cook 2½ hours

A very nice lady called Cath does all the figures at Ella's Kitchen. She's also a dessert queen and has created this variation on a traditional rice pudding.

What you need

2 tablespoons **unsalted butter**

⅔ cup **short-grain rice**

¼ cup firmly packed **light brown sugar**

1¾ cups canned **coconut milk**

1¼ cups **light cream**

2½ cups **whole milk**

1 teaspoon **vanilla extract**

A pinch of **ground cinnamon**

For the mango sauce

1 (15-ounce) can **sliced mangoes**

¼ cup **apple juice**

2 tablespoons **honey**

Milk and cream

Ask your little helpers to taste a little spoon of coconut milk and then a little spoon of cream. Talk about the different tastes and textures they have and the different places that they come from.

What to do

1. Preheat the oven to 300°F and grease a 12 x 8-inch ovenproof dish with a little of the butter.

2. Spread the rice evenly over the bottom of the dish. Sprinkle the sugar on top.

3. Pour the coconut milk into a separate bowl and use a wire whisk to mix it up thoroughly. Add the cream, milk, and vanilla extract and mix again.

4. Pour the coconut milk mixture over the rice and sugar, sprinkle with the cinnamon, and dot the top with the remaining butter. Put the dish in the center of the oven and bake for 2½ hours, until the top is golden brown.

5. While the rice pudding is cooking, prepare the mango sauce. Strain the mangoes and discard the syrup. Reserve two of the mango slices. Puree the remaining mango in a food processor or with a handheld immersion blender until smooth. Add the apple juice and honey and mix well. Cut the reserved mango slices into ½-inch chunks and add them to the sauce.

6. Serve the rice pudding hot or cold with the mango sauce spooned on top.

Berry nice blueberry cream

Blueberries proved a definite hit with our pint-size tasters. You can also make this fuss-free, creamy sundae for breakfast, if you prefer.

What you need

1 cup **crème fraîche** or **vanilla-flavor yogurt**

1¼ cups **Greek yogurt**

Finely grated rind and juice of 1 **lemon**

2 cups **blueberries**

1 tablespoon **honey**

Confectioners' sugar, for dusting

What to do

1. Put the crème fraîche in a mixing bowl with the Greek yogurt and fold through the grated lemon rind. Divide one-third of the mixture among four serving glasses.

2. Reserve a few blueberries for decoration. Put the remaining blueberries into a bowl with 1 tablespoon of lemon juice and the honey. Lightly mash with a potato masher, just until a few blueberries have burst, but most still remain whole. Stir the mixture well.

3. Divide half the blueberry among between the glasses in an even layer on top of the crème fraîche mixture. Then top with another third of the crème fraîche mixture, the remaining blueberry mixture, and then finally the last third of the crème fraîche mixture.

4. Decorate the top of the sundae with a few of the reserved blueberries and dust with confectioners' sugar to serve.

One for you

One for me

Smiley spiral apple tarts

Who knew apple tarts could taste this good? Little ones will love to get involved using pastry cutters and decorating the tarts with apple slices.

What you need

1 sheet store-bought **puff pastry**

2 crisp **apples** (Granny Smith or Royal Gala work best)

1 tablespoon **lemon juice**

4 tablespoons **unsalted butter**, cut into 6 pats

½ teaspoon **ground cinnamon**

2 tablespoons packed **light brown sugar**

Roll, cut, fill

Can I help?

Tots of all ages get to play at being baker with these simple apple tarts. Making them is a great activity for a play date. One friend rolls the dough, another cuts the circles, and another fills the tart with pieces of apple.

What to do

1. Preheat the oven to 400°F.

2. Roll out the puff pastry until it is ¼-in thick. Using a 4-inch pastry cutter, cut out six circles from the pastry and place them spaced well apart on a baking sheet.

3. Core the apples, then cut them into very thin slices and put them in a bowl with the lemon juice. Toss the apple slices well to coat them in the juice. Arrange the apple slices on top of the dough circles in a "flower" pattern.

4. Place a pat of butter on each tart, then sprinkle the tarts with a little cinnamon (to taste) and the sugar.

5. Bake the tarts in the oven for 15–20 minutes, until golden brown. Serve them warm or cold with vanilla ice cream, whipped cream, or Greek yogurt.

Wonderful watermelon ice

serves 8–10
prep 20 minutes + freezing

A kind of kiddie granita, this is the ultimate zingy-fresh slushie. The freezing and scraping process to make the ice slush is all part of the fun.

What you need

6 cups cubed **watermelon** flesh, (about 4 pounds watermelon, peeled and seeds removed)

¼ cup **granulated sugar**

Juice of 1 **lime**

Get ahead

You can make this icy dessert up to three days before you need it. Keep it in the freezer with the lid on the container, or tightly covered with aluminum foil. To serve, first give it a quick scrape and a mash with a fork.

Save the seeds!

Don't throw away the seeds from your watermelon—dried-out seeds are great for making shakers or using as "money" in a game of stores. Rinse the discarded seeds in water and then lay them out on paper towels in a warm place for 7–10 days. The seeds are completely dry when they snap instead of bend between your fingers.

What to do

1. Put all the ingredients in a food processor and process until smooth (you can put everything in a bowl and use a handheld immersion blender if you don't have a food processor).

2. Pour the mixture into a shallow freezer container, put the lid on, and freeze the mixture for 1 hour.

3. Remove the mixture from the freezer and stir it well, mashing any frozen parts with the back of a fork.

4. Replace the lid and freeze the mixture for another 2 hours, until firm.

5. Using a fork, scrape the frozen mixture vigorously to form icy flakes. Serve in plastic cups or small glasses.

Color me in

Zingy pineapple with basil + lime

These ingredients sound grown up, but we've found that older toddlers are interested to find out about the zesty tastes and textures—and then love them when they dig in.

What you need

Finely grated rind and juice of 1 **lime**

¼ cup firmly packed **dark brown sugar**

1 tablespoon finely chopped **basil** leaves, plus extra for decorating

1 whole **pineapple**, peeled, cored, and cut into sticks

What to do

1. Place the lime rind and juice in a bowl and stir in the sugar and basil. Let the mixture marinate for 5 minutes, until the sugar has dissolved to form a syrup.

2. Arrange the pineapple sticks on a large serving plate and drizzle with some of the lime-and-basil syrup. Put any remaining syrup in a little bowl for extra dunking. Serve immediately.

Smell-a-thon

Crushing the basil releases its delicious smell—talk to your toddler about it and what it might remind you of. Summertime? Pizza? And what about the smell of the lime? How is that different from the pineapple?

Make it mango

As an alternative, you can substitute the pineapple with 2 fresh mangoes, pitted, peeled, and sliced, for a different kind of tropical flavor.

Dip me in

Fabulous fruit compote

You can enjoy this versatile fruit compote for breakfast served with yogurt and granola, as a hot or cold snack, or for a dinner-time dessert served with ice cream or yogurt.

What you need

2 sweet crisp **apples**, peeled, cored, and diced

2 **Bosc pears**, peeled, cored, and diced

6 **plums**, pitted and diced

10 **dried prunes**, coarsely chopped

⅓ cup **golden raisins**

Finely grated rind and juice of 1 **orange**

½ teaspoon **allspice**

What to do

1) Place all the ingredients in a medium saucepan, cover with a lid, and cook gently for 20 minutes, stirring occasionally, until the fruit has softened but there is still some texture.

2) Remove the pan from the heat. Serve the compote warm or cold.

Hello...

134

Tasty treats

Hello!
How many bananas
can you spot in
this chapter?
Love, Ella x

Teeny weeny fruit muffins

makes **12** · prep **20** minutes · cook **20** minutes

The fruit puree makes these muffins *reeeally* moist. The muffins are a cinch to make and bake in 20 minutes, so provide a perfect afternoon cooking activity when a friend comes to play. Mmmm ... warm muffins to keep them going until dinner. Perfect.

What you need

5 tablespoons **unsalted butter**, softened

¼ cup **granulated sugar**

1 **egg**

⅔ cup **whole-wheat flour**

1 teaspoon **baking powder**

1 cup hulled **strawberries** or **raspberries**, pureed (reserve a few whole berries)

⅓ cup **raisins**

½ cup finely **chopped walnuts** (optional)

Rolled oats, to sprinkle

What to do

1. Preheat the oven to 350°F. Line a mini muffin pan with cupcake paper liners.

2. Cream together the butter and sugar in a large bowl until light and fluffy. Add the egg and stir in well to combine. Sift in the flour and baking powder and stir again. Finally, stir in the pureed strawberry or raspberry and the raisins, then the walnuts (if using).

3. Divide the batter between the paper liners, filling each about three-quarters full so that the muffins have room to rise. Sprinkle a few rolled oats over each muffin.

4. Bake for 20 minutes, until the muffins are firm to the touch and golden brown on top.

5. Cool them on a wire rack before serving. They will keep in an airtight container for up to 3 days.

Can I help?

Bake away!

This is a baking extravaganza for tiny helpers. Little ones can help out with the creaming, cracking eggs, sifting, stirring, and sprinkling—there's so much to do, and so much messy fun to be had.

Ella's shortcut

To save time, you can replace the pureed strawberries or raspberries with 1 (3-ounce) pouch of Ella's Kitchen Smoothie Fruits—The Red One.

Rise 'n' shine banana bread

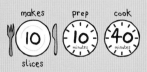

makes 10 slices · prep 10 minutes · cook 40 minutes

This simple banana bread is deliciously moist and ideal for a late breakfast, as a morning snack for a trip to the park, or with a cup of juice as an afternoon snack.

What you need

3 very ripe **bananas**

2 tablespoons **apple juice**

1 stick **unsalted butter**, plus extra for greasing

2 **eggs**

2 cups **all-purpose flour**

2 teaspoons **baking powder**

What to do

1. Preheat the oven to 350°F. Lightly grease a 9 x 5 x 3-inch loaf pan.

2. Mash the bananas, using a fork, add the apple juice, and stir to combine.

3. Cream the butter until light and fluffy, then beat in the eggs, one at a time, and mix well. Fold in the flour until fully combined, then fold in the mashed banana-and-apple mixture.

4. Turn the mixture into the prepared pan. Bake for about 40 minutes, until golden. Test the loaf by piercing it with a toothpick: it should come out clean.

5. Let the loaf cool slightly, then turn it out onto a wire rack to cool completely. Cut it into slices to serve.

Choccie chocolate munchies

makes **16** squares

prep **25** minutes + chilling

This is a favorite with all little cookie monsters and there's no baking required, which means that they can get involved in every stage of the making ... as well as the eating!

What you need

7 ounces **butter** or **plain cookies**

1 stick **unsalted butter**, plus extra for greasing

3 tablespoons **light corn syrup**

2 tablespoons **unsweetened cocoa powder**

⅓ cup **raisins**

4 ounces **semisweet chocolate**, broken into pieces

Munchie making

Can I help?

Get your little ones involved in the cookie bashing in this recipe. Ask for help breaking up the chocolate and cleaning up the chocolate bowl.

What to do

1. Butter a 7-inch cake pan. Either seal the cookies inside a strong plastic bag or place them in a large plastic bowl. Pound the cookies with a rolling pin to bash them up into uneven crumbs.

2. Melt the butter and corn syrup in a saucepan. Stir in the cocoa powder and raisins, then thoroughly stir in the cookie crumbs. Spoon the mixture into the prepared pan and press down firmly all over. Put the mixture in the refrigerator to chill for 10 minutes.

3. Meanwhile, melt the chocolate pieces in a double boiler or a heatproof bowl set over a saucepan of simmering water (or melt the chocolate in a microwave on medium for 2–3 minutes). Remove the cookie mixture from the refrigerator and spread the melted chocolate over it. Return it to the refrigerator to chill for another 30 minutes, until firm and set.

4. Remove the firm munchie mixture from the pan, put it on a cutting board, and cut it into 16 squares. You can store the munchies in an airtight container in the refrigerator for up to a week.

How high can I go?

Nicely spicy veggie chips

Kids love crunchy snacks and our healthy alternative to standard potato chips has extra veggie goodness without losing any of the munchiness.

What you need

2 **parsnips**

1 **sweet potato**

1 raw **beet**

2 tablespoons **olive oil**

¼ teaspoon **mild chili powder**

What to do

1. Preheat the oven to 425°F.

2. Using a potato peeler or mandoline (be careful), slice the vegetables on the diagonal very thinly to create wafer-thin chips, about ¹⁄₁₆ inch thick. Spread out the vegetable slices on paper towels to draw out any excess moisture.

3. Place the parsnips and sweet potato slices into a bowl with 1 tablespoon of the olive oil and the chili powder and toss to lightly coat, then spread them out on a baking sheet. Place the beet slices into a bowl with the remaining oil and toss well. Spread out the beet slices on another baking sheet.

4. Roast all the vegetables in the center of the preheated oven for 20 minutes, turning them halfway through cooking, if necessary, until they are crisp.

5. Remove the baking sheets from the oven and spread out the vegetable chips on paper towels to cool slightly before serving. Eat immediately.

5 ways

Five ways with popcorn

Popcorn is a great weekend treat that all the family can enjoy—ideally in front of a favorite movie.

serves 4

prep 5 minutes

cook 5 minutes

Basic popcorn recipe

²⁄₃ cup **popping corn**

Put the popping corn in a very large saucepan and place it over high heat, covered with a lid.

Holding the lid, cook the popcorn for about 3–5 minutes, until it begins to pop. It will pop repeatedly and then finally stop popping altogether. Shake the pan continuously throughout the process to keep it moving.

Turn off the heat and remove the lid from the pan to let the popcorn cool a little before adding the flavoring of your choice.

Cheesy popcorn

1 quantity basic **popcorn** (above)

1 cup grated **Parmesan cheese**

½ teaspoon **mild chili powder** (optional)

Sprinkle the Parmesan, in batches, over the freshly cooked, warm popcorn, shaking the pan gently and stirring through each batch of cheese before adding the next. Keep going until all the popcorn is lightly covered and the cheese has melted a little.

Sprinkle over ½ teaspoon mild chili powder (if using) before serving.

Bacon-flavored popcorn

1 quantity basic **popcorn**
  (opposite)

4 tablespoons **unsalted butter**

4 ounces **unsmoked bacon**,
  finely shredded

Heat the butter in a large skillet and gently cook the bacon for 2–3 minutes, until just beginning to crisp.

Once the popcorn has cooked, pour in the butter-and-bacon mixture and toss with the popcorn until lightly covered. Serve warm.

Caramel popcorn

1 quantity basic **popcorn**
  (opposite)

4 tablespoons **unsalted butter**

2 tablespoons packed **light
  brown sugar**

2 tablespoons **heavy cream**

Heat the butter in a small saucepan, then add the sugar and stir well for about 2 minutes, until the sugar dissolves.

Remove the pan from the heat and add the cream, stirring well until a caramel has formed. Pour it over the freshly cooked popcorn and gently toss to lightly coat.

Peanut butter popcorn

1 quantity basic **popcorn** (opposite)

2 tablespoons **unsalted butter**

2 tablespoons packed **light
  brown sugar**

3 tablespoons **smooth peanut
  butter**

Heat the butter in a large saucepan, then add the sugar and stir well for about 2 minutes, until the sugar dissolves. Stir in the peanut butter.

Add the cooked popcorn to the pan with the peanut butter mixture, in batches, and gently toss to lightly coat.

Cinnamon popcorn

1 quantity basic **popcorn**
  (opposite)

4 tablespoons **unsalted butter**

2 tablespoons **coarse raw sugar**

½ teaspoon **ground cinnamon**

Heat the butter in a small saucepan, then add the sugar and cinnamon and stir well for about 2 minutes, until the sugar dissolves.

Pour the cinnamon mixture over the freshly made popcorn and gently toss to lightly coat.

Mix + match crumbly cookies

makes 20–24 | prep 30 minutes + chilling | cook 10 minutes

This cookie-dough combination was made to inspire budding designers. From splats to braids and from rocks to rolls, let imaginations go wild and little fingers get messy!

What you need

1½ sticks **unsalted butter**

¾ cup **granulated sugar**

1 teaspoon **vanilla extract**

1 **egg**

1⅔ cups **all-purpose flour**

1 teaspoon **baking powder**

2 tablespoons **unsweetened cocoa powder**

1 tablespoon finely grated **orange** rind

Cookie art

Rolling, squashing, and cutting the cookie dough are cooking activities simply made for tiny hands. Get the kids involved all the way through with this one.

What to do

1. Preheat the oven to 350°F.

2. In a medium bowl, cream together the butter, sugar, and vanilla extract until smooth. Beat in the egg. In a separate bowl, combine the flour and baking powder, then stir the dry ingredients into the butter-and-sugar mixture. Combine until you have a soft dough.

3. Divide the dough in half. Add the cocoa powder to one half, kneading the dough until it is completely chocolatey. Add the orange rind to the remaining dough, kneading it through as before.

4. Place each piece of dough onto a well-floured surface and, using your hands, create cylindrical rope shapes of about 12 inches long from each type of dough. Lay 1 chocolate and 1 orange dough cylinder side by side and, beginning at one end, turn the cylinders to create a spiral. Repeat for all the dough cylinders.

5. Place your combined dough pieces onto a baking sheet and freeze for 10 minutes until firm. When chilled, flatten each wheel with a rolling pin, then use cookie cutters to cut two-tone shapes from the dough.

6. Place the cookies, spaced well apart, onto a large baking sheet lined with parchment paper and bake for 8–10 minutes, until cooked through. Cool on a wire rack.

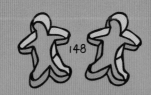

Awesome orange and ginger cake

This cake is a sweet and yummy introduction to ginger—have fun helping your little ones discover new tastes for their developing taste buds.

What you need

5 tablespoons **unsalted butter**

⅔ cup **light corn syrup** or ½ cup **molasses**

1¾ cups **all-purpose flour**

1¾ teaspoons **baking powder**

2 teaspoons **ground ginger**

1 teaspoon **ground cinnamon**

¾ cup **orange marmalade**

1 **egg**, beaten

1 tablespoon freshly squeezed **orange juice**

What to do

1. Preheat the oven to 350°F. Grease an 8-inch square cake pan and line the bottom with parchment paper.

2. Melt the butter and syrup in a saucepan over low heat, stirring well to combine. Remove the mixture from the heat and set aside.

3. Sift the flour, baking powder, ginger, and cinnamon into a bowl, then slowly pour the syrup mixture into the flour mixture and stir to combine. Add the marmalade, egg, orange juice, and 1 tablespoon of hot water and combine to make a soft mixture. Add another 1–2 tablespoons of hot water if it is too stiff.

4. Pour the batter into the cake pan and spread evenly. Bake the cake for 30–35 minutes, until golden brown and firm to the touch.

5. Let the cake cool for 15 minutes in the pan before carefully transferring it to a wire rack. Serve it warm with a scoop of vanilla ice cream, or cold with a glass of freshly squeezed orange juice.

I might be a little too hot for your pocket!

Pizza pocket bites

makes **8** · prep **20** minutes · cook **25** minutes
+ proving

These are no ordinary bread rolls—they're bite-size and have pizza flavors buried in the center to tantalize the taste buds. Eat them on their own or as an accompaniment to pasta dishes. You can omit the pepperoni for a veggie alternative.

What you need

2 (6½-ounce) boxes **pizza-crust mix**

2 tablespoons finely chopped **oregano**

1 tablespoon **olive oil**

¼ each small **red**, **yellow**, and **green bell pepper**, sliced

1¾ ounces **pepperoni**, roughly chopped

1 cup grated **cheddar cheese** or **mozzarella cheese**

Kneading time

Can I help?

Your toddler can help you to knead the veggies into the dough pieces and roll them into balls—great foody play that helps to get the job done!

What to do

1. Preheat the oven to 425°F.

2. Put the pizza-crust dough in a bowl with the oregano, add the required amount of warm water according to the package directions, and mix thoroughly to form a smooth dough.

3. Turn out the dough onto a lightly floured surface and knead it until it is smooth.

4. Heat the oil in a heavy skillet and cook the bell peppers over moderate heat for 4–5 minutes, until soft, then add the pepperoni and cook for another 1 minute.

5. Divide the dough into eight pieces and make a well in the center of each. Divide the bell peppers and pepperoni among the dough pieces and very coarsely knead them into the dough, then shape the dough pieces into coarse balls and place them on a baking sheet. Cover the balls with a damp cloth and let them rise for 30 minutes, or until they have roughly doubled in size.

6. Sprinkle the balls with the cheese and bake them for 20 minutes, until they are golden brown and cooked through—when they're cooked, the bottom of each pizza bite should sound hollow when you tap it. Serve the pizza bites while they are still warm.

153

Flour dough fun

Our special cloud dough is so much fun—and best of all, it's supereasy to make. It's also messy, so give everyone an apron and cover the table before you get started.

1

Mix it up

In a bowl, mix together 8 cups of cornstarch and 1–2 cups of vegetable oil. Work it all together to combine. Little fingers dig in right away— getting messy is all part of the fun.

2

Add the sparkle

Add in a few sprinkles of glitter and mix them through. Now it's like fairy dust! The dough should hold together when molded gently, but crumble away if you apply pressure.

Watch the magic

When it's all fully mixed together, it's time to play. Put the cloud dough into a large baking sheet, then mold it into shapes—a little like building sparkly sandcastles. When you're ready, knock them down and build some more!

Magic goop

When you've had enough of cloud dough, try magic goop instead. In a big bowl, mix together 4 cups cornstarch and 2 cups of water. Add food coloring—the brighter the better, but be careful, because it may stain your clothes. Then, watch! At first the goop feels firm, but suddenly it will stream through little fingers like magic. Make your goop sparkle by adding some twinkly glitter; or make it smell delicious with a drop or two of peppermint essence.

Cheesy straw dippers

We think these are the flakiest, cheesiest, most perfect cheese straws we've ever tasted. They taste even better when they're dunked in our cheesy pesto dip.

What you need

4 tablespoons **unsalted butter**, softened

2 cups grated **cheddar cheese**

1 cup **whole-wheat flour**

1 **egg**, lightly beaten

2 tablespoons **sesame seeds**

¼ teaspoon **mild chili powder** or **paprika**

For the pesto dip

2 tablespoons **pesto** or our **Green Pasta Sauce** (see page 96)

¼ cup **cream cheese**

2 tablespoons **whole milk**

What to do

1. Preheat the oven to 400°F.

2. In a food processor, cream together the butter and cheese. Stir in the flour and form the mixture into a soft dough.

3. On a lightly floured surface, roll out the dough until it is about ⅝ inch thick. Brush the flattened dough with the beaten egg, then cut it into 2-inch strips. Sprinkle the strips with the sesame seeds and chili powder or paprika.

4. Put the strips on a lightly greased baking sheet and bake them for 10–15 minutes, until crisp.

5. Meanwhile, make the pesto dip by mixing the pesto or Green Pasta Sauce with the cream cheese and milk until fully combined. Put the dip in a small dipping bowl and serve with the warm cheese straws.

Rollin' rollin' rollin'

Can I help?

Lightly flour your surface, put down your ball of cheesy dough, and let your little helper roll away. Once the dough is flat, he or she can brush over the egg glaze, too.

Carroty cakes

Carrots make a wonderfully moist cake. These little treats are especially good because the decorations are made from real carrot shavings.

What you need

3 **carrots**

¾ cup packed **light brown sugar**

1⅔ cups **all-purpose flour**

1½ teaspoons **baking powder**

1 teaspoon **baking soda**

2 teaspoons **ground cinnamon**

Finely grated rind of 1 **orange**

2 **eggs**, beaten

⅔ cup **sunflower oil**

For the topping

4 tablespoons **unsalted butter**, softened

⅔ cup **confectioners' sugar**

½ cup **cream cheese**

Carrot shavings, to decorate (optional)

What to do

1. Preheat the oven to 350°F. Grease a 7-inch square cake pan.

2. Shred the carrots finely into a large mixing bowl. Sift the sugar, flour, baking powder, baking soda, and cinnamon on top of the carrot, then add the orange rind and mix everything together. Add the eggs and the oil to the mixture. Mix everything together well.

3. Spoon the batter into the cake pan and level the top. Bake for 30 minutes or until the cake is cooked through—test it by piercing it with a toothpick. It should come out clean. Remove the cake from the oven and let cool in the pan placed on a wire rack.

4. Meanwhile, make the topping. Mix together the butter and confectioners' sugar, then stir in the cream cheese until smooth.

5. When the cake is cool, carefully turn it out onto a board. Spread the topping evenly over the cake and cut the cake into 16 squares. Decorate each square with a shaving of fresh carrot, if you like.

Beautiful breakfasts

Everyone loves a lazy weekend breakfast—
especially if it occasionally turns into lunch!
Here are some tasty ideas for leisurely breakfasts
that little ones can get involved in making themselves—
with a little bit of supervision from the grown-ups.

Very berry smoothie

serves **4**   prep **5** minutes

Full of fruity goodness and great for slurping, this smoothie is always a hit.

⅓ cup **vanilla yogurt**

1½ cups **frozen berries** or **fresh fruit** (mango, pineapple, raspberries, or whatever is in season)

1 ripe **banana**

⅔ cup **fruit juice** (any flavor)

Place all the ingredients into a food processor and process until smooth. Pour into four glasses and serve immediately.

What color?

Before you blend up the fruit, you can try guessing what color the smoothie is going to be. Talk about the colors of the individual fruits and then older toddlers can try to predict the result.

Purple pancakes

Who said pancakes have to be yellow? Squashed blueberries added to the batter make pancakes that are purple—a special surprise for the weekend.

1¼ cups **all-purpose flour**

1¼ teaspoons **baking soda**

1 **egg**

⅔ cup **whole milk**

⅓ cup **blueberries**

Unsalted butter, for frying

Maple syrup, to serve (optional)

Fresh fruit, to serve (optional)

Sift the flour and baking soda into a small mixing bowl and make a well in the center.

Break the egg into a small bowl, add the milk, and mix well. Pour the mixture into the well and, using a wire whisk, draw the flour into the liquid gradually and mix it all together until combined to a smooth batter.

Place the blueberries in a small bowl and, using a handheld immersion blender, blend until almost smooth and very purple!

Pour the purple puree into the pancake batter and mix well.

Wipe the bottom of a large, heavy skillet with a little butter and heat. Pour large spoonfuls of the batter, spaced well apart, into the the skillet and cook the pancakes for about 1 minute, then flip them over, using a spatula, and cook on the other side for another 30 seconds–1 minute, until golden brown on both sides.

Remove the pancakes from the skillet and keep them warm. Repeat the process until all the batter is used. Serve the pancakes warm with a little maple syrup and fresh fruit (if using).

Getting it level

Can I help?

Measuring the blueberries is a good introduction to using measuring cups for little ones—and less messy than measuring flour or sugar!

Holey moley pancakes

This pancake variation is courtesy of Kim, who runs our Making Friends team here at Ella's Kitchen. She loves to make them with her nieces and nephews when they come to stay. The little holes are the secret to a great pancake taste experience.

1 cup **all-purpose flour**

½ teaspoon **baking soda**

½ teaspoon **cream of tartar**

1 **egg**

1 tablespoon **sugar**

2 tablespoons **unsalted butter**, melted, plus extra for frying

⅔ cup **whole milk**

Fresh fruit, to serve (optional)

Mix the flour with the baking soda and cream of tartar. In a separate bowl, cream the egg and sugar, then stir in the melted butter. Then, alternately add small amounts of the flour mixture and the milk to the egg mixture until everything is combined to a thick batter.

Wipe the bottom of a large, heavy skillet with a little butter and heat. Spoon in individual tablespoons of the batter to form small pancakes. Cook for about 1 minute, until the bubbles have burst, then flip the pancakes over, using a spatula, and cook for another 30 seconds, until golden brown on both sides.

Remove the pancakes from the skillet and keep them warm. Repeat the process until all the batter is used. Serve the pancakes warm with fresh fruit (if using).

Strawberry, banana + mango oatmeal

This deliciously fruity oatmeal is just about the perfect start to the day—a warming breakfast that the whole family will want to try!

1 large **banana**, coarsely chopped

1 cup hulled and coarsely chopped **strawberries**

½ **mango**, coarsely chopped

1½ tablespoons **honey**

½ teaspoon **ground cinnamon**

2½ cups **whole milk**

1⅔ cup **rolled oats**

Place the fruit in a saucepan with the honey, cinnamon, and 2 tablespoons of water. Bring to a boil, stir gently to combine, and cook over medium heat for 3–4 minutes, until the fruit is soft and a toffeelike sauce has formed.

In a separate saucepan, bring the milk to a boil, stirring occasionally, then remove it from the heat and add the rolled oats. Stir well, then return the pan to low heat, stirring continuously, for 5–6 minutes, until the oatmeal has thickened.

Stir half the fruit mixture through the oatmeal and mix well, then ladle the fruity oatmeal into warmed serving bowls and spoon the remaining fruit over the top.

Slowly, slowly stirring

Can I help?

Older children can help you stir the oatmeal slowly—but keep a very attentive eye on them the whole time. Talk about how the mixture changes from runny to thick.

5 ways

Five ways with eggs

Lazy weekend breakfasts are made for sharing. We love that the humble egg lets us rustle up so many tastes and textures.

Scrambled egg + avocado

serves 2-4 | prep 5 minutes | cook 5 minutes

4 **eggs**, beaten

Unsalted butter, for frying

¼ cup **crème fraîche** or **heavy cream**

1 small **avocado**, coarsely chopped

¼ teaspoon **paprika**

Freshly ground **black pepper**

Place the eggs in a small, heavy saucepan with the butter and cook them over low heat, stirring continuously, until the eggs begin to cook.

Remove the eggs from the heat, season with a little pepper, then add the crème fraîche. Return the mixture to the heat and cook, stirring continuously, until the egg is cooked through but the mixture is still soft.

Remove the eggs from the heat, stir in the avocado and paprika ,and serve with whole-wheat toast.

Lemon soufflé cloud omelet

serves 2 | prep 5 minutes | cook 4 minutes

3 **eggs**, separated

Finely grated rind and juice of 1 **lemon**

1 tablespoon **superfine sugar**

Unsalted butter, for frying

1 teaspoon **confectioner' sugar**

Whisk the egg whites until stiff. In a separate bowl, mix together the egg yolks, lemon juice and rind, and superfine sugar.

Heat the butter in a medium skillet. Fold together the egg whites and yolk mixture, then pour it all into the skillet.

Cook the omelet over gentle heat for 2–3 minutes on one side, then flip it over and cook the other side for about 30 seconds, until both sides are just golden bown.

Turn the omelet out of the skillet onto a warmed plate and sprinkle with confectioners' sugar.

Cheesy scramble

serves **4**   prep **5** minutes   cook **4** minutes

Unsalted butter, for frying

4 **eggs**

¼ cup **whole milk**

⅔ cup grated **American cheese** or **cheddar cheese**

Heat the butter in a small, heavy saucepan over low heat.

Beat the eggs, milk, and cheese with a wooden spoon, then pour into the skillet.

Stir continuously over the heat for 3–4 minutes, until the eggs are softly scrambled and cooked through and the cheese has melted.

Serve on a slice of toasted whole-wheat or sourdough bread, if liked.

Ham + egg muffins

serves **4**   prep **5** minutes   cook **5** minutes

4 **eggs**

2 **muffins**, halved and toasted

4 thick slices good-quality **ham**

¼ cup **hollandaise sauce**

To poach the eggs, bring a small saucepan of lightly salted water to a boil. Stir the water briskly to create a whirlpool and then crack the eggs into it, one or two at a time, and cook for 2–3 minutes. Remove the eggs from the pan, using a slotted spoon, and keep warm.

Lightly toast the muffins and place each toasted half on a warmed serving plate. Top with a slice of ham and a poached egg. Spoon 1 tablespoon of hollandaise sauce over each egg to serve.

Cinnamon French toast

serves **4**   prep **5** minutes   cook **2–3** minutes

2 **eggs**, beaten

½ cup **whole milk**

1 teaspoon **ground cinnamon**

4 slices **brioche**

Unsalted butter, for frying

4 teaspoons **coarse raw sugar** or **granulated sugar**

Place the eggs in a small bowl with the milk and ½ teaspoon of the cinnamon and beat together. Dip the brioche slices into the milk mixture, letting it soak in a little. Melt the butter in a large, heavy skillet, then cook the egg-coated brioche slices over high heat for 1–2 minutes on each side, until lightly golden brown. Mix the raw sugar with the remaining cinnamon and sprinkle it over the French toast.

For a special treat, why not have a day dedicated to chocolate! Have fun experimenting with different combinations of fruit and chocolate, or try making the best chocolate cake ever. There's nothing quite like the gooey, chocolatey mess that happens when you dig in!

Warm chocolate pots

serves 6 | prep 5 minutes | cook 5 minutes

This is a yummy cross between chocolate mousse and chocolate pudding and we dare anyone not to like it! It's ideal for chocolate moustaches.

10 ounces **semisweet chocolate**, broken up	
2 cups **fromage blanc**, or 1 cup **cottage cheese** mixed with 1 cup **plain** or **Greek yogurt**	
1 teaspoon **vanilla extract**	
unsweetened cocoa powder, for dusting (optional)	

Melt the chocolate in a bowl over a saucepan of gently simmering water. When the chocolate has melted, remove the pan from the heat.

Take the bowl off the pan and add the fromage blanc and vanilla extract, quickly stirring it all together until the ingredients are fully combined.

Divide the mixture among little pots, cups, or glasses. Dust with cocoa powder (if using) and serve immediately.

Fruity fun choccie dippers

serves 4 | prep 5 minutes | cook 10 minutes

Delicious pieces of fruit dunked in three kinds of chocolate—lip-smackingly good!

8 ounces **milk chocolate**, broken up	
8 ounces **semisweet chocolate**, broken up	
8 ounces **white chocolate**, broken up	
Slices of **apple**, **pear**, **melon**, and **pineapple**, halved **grapes**, and whole **strawberries**, for dunking	

Put the pieces of milk, semisweet, and white chocolate into three separate bowls.

In turn, place each bowl over a saucepan of gently simmering water and melt the three types of chocolate until each becomes smooth, glossy, and runny.

Transfer each type of chocolate into its own serving dish and serve immediately with bowls of the fruit on the side for dunking.

Best-ever chocolate cake

serves 10 | prep 20 minutes | cook 40–50 minutes

Whether it be for a birthday or other celebration, or a simple afternoon snack, every family needs a best-ever chocolate cake recipe. Listen for the chorus of "More, please!"

1¼ cups **all-purpose flour**

½ cup good-quality unsweetened **cocoa powder**

1 heaping teaspoon **baking powder**

1½ sticks **unsalted butter**, softened

⅔ cup firmly packed **light brown sugar**

3 **eggs**, beaten

1 cup **sour cream**

1 teaspoon **vanilla extract**

For the frosting

4 ounces **semisweet chocolate**, broken up

1½ sticks **unsalted butter**, softened

½ cup **cream cheese**

1⅓ cups **confectioners' sugar**, sifted

2 ounces **milk**, **semisweet**, and **white chocolate**, grated, to decorate

Preheat the oven to 350°F. Grease an 8-inch springform cake pan and line it with parchment paper.

Sift the flour, cocoa powder, and baking powder into a bowl. In a separate bowl, cream together the butter and brown sugar until light and fluffy. A little at a time, add the beaten eggs with a spoonful of the flour mixture to the butter mixture, stirring continuously.

Add in the remaining flour mixture along with the sour cream and vanilla extract and fold everything together, using a metal spoon. Spoon the cake batter into the prepared pan and bake for 40–50 minutes, until the cake has risen and is firm to the touch. The cake is ready when a toothpick inserted into the center comes out clean. Let the cake cool in the pan for about 20 minutes, then turn it out onto a wire rack to cool completely.

Meanwhile make the frosting. Melt the chocolate in a bowl set over a saucepan of gently simmering water. Once it has melted, set it aside to cool. In a separate bowl, beat the butter and cream cheese with a wooden spoon until combined. Beat in the confectioners' sugar, then the cooled chocolate, being careful not to overbeat.

Cut the cooked cake in half horizontally and use one-third of the frosting to sandwich the two pieces together. Transfer the cake to a serving board or plate and cover the top and sides with the remaining frosting. Decorate with the grated chocolate.

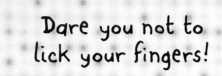

The smell of homemade pizza baking in the oven is definitely wonderful. Transforming your kitchen into a pizza cafe means there's plenty for everyone to do—from creating the menus and taking the orders to preparing the pizza dough and arranging the toppings. Have fun!

Potato pizza

serves **4** | prep **25** minutes | cook **20** minutes
+ proving

¾ cup **all-purpose flour**

¼ teaspoon **active dry yeast**

2 teaspoons **sugar**

⅓ cup mashed **potatoes**

1 **egg**, beaten

⅓ cup **pizza sauce** or **Great Tomato Sauce** (see page 32)

6 **sun-dried tomatoes**

½ cup grated **mozzarella cheese**

Basil leaves, to serve

In a small bowl, combine the flour, yeast, and sugar. Add the mashed potatoes and mix. The dough should look clumpy. Add 3 tablespoons of water and then the egg and stir with a spatula until the mixture forms a loose dough.

Knead the dough on a lightly floured surface until it becomes smooth. Put it in a bowl, cover the bowl with a damp dish towel, and set the dough aside to rise for 30 minutes in a warm place.

Preheat the oven to 400°F.

Knead the dough again on a lightly floured surface and roll it out to a circle measuring about 8 inches in diameter. Place it on a large baking sheet. Lightly cover the dough with a dish towel and let rest for another 15 minutes. After this time, spread the dough with the pizza sauce or Great Tomato Sauce, tomatoes, and mozzarella.

Bake the pizza in the preheated oven for 20 minutes, until the mozzarella is bubbling and golden. Sprinkle the pizza with basil leaves and serve cut into wedges. (Try some of the other topping suggestions on page 179, too.)

175

Roaring arugula pizza

serves **4**   prep **5** minutes   cook **8–10** minutes

This is the quickest pizza ever, and the arugula adds some greens. Children love the stringiness of the mozzarella.

4 small round **whole-wheat pita breads**

¼ cup **concentrated tomato paste** or **Great Tomato Sauce** (see page 32)

4 ounces **mozzarella cheese**, cut into slices (or 4 handfuls of grated mozzarella)

2 handfuls of **arugula** leaves

Preheat the oven to 425°F.

Place the pita breads on a baking sheet and spread each pita evenly with the tomato paste or Great Tomato Sauce, then cover each with mozzarella.

Bake the pizzas in the middle of the oven for 8–10 minutes, or until the cheese is melted and has turned golden brown.

Let the cooked pizzas cool for a few minutes, then sprinkle with arugula leaves and serve immediately.

Pesto pizza?

You can vary the toppings and also the sauce. Instead of the puree or Great Tomato Sauce, try spreading each pita bread with 2 teaspoons of tomato pesto from a jar.

Color me in

Topping the pie

Can I help?

Spreading over delicious helpings of tomato paste with a plastic knife, or with a butter knife that has a blunt end, is a great way for children to get involved. They can sprinkle their own toppings over the top, too.

Biscuit pizza

serves 6 | prep 15 minutes | cook 25 minutes

Pizzas don't have to be round. Use a cookie cutter to create your favorite shape. Choose your toppings. Adding herbs to the biscuit mixture in these pizzas makes for extra tastiness.

4 cups **all-purpose flour**	
4 teaspoons **baking powder**	
1 cup **ricotta cheese**	
1 **egg**	
3 tablespoons finely chopped mixed **fresh herbs** (such as basil, parsley, and oregano)	
4 **sun-dried tomatoes**, drained and coarsely chopped	
1 cup **whole milk**	
¼ cup **tomato paste** or **Great Tomato Sauce** (see page 32)	
¾ cup pitted **black olives**, coarsely chopped	
½ cup finely chopped **mozzarella cheese**	
Freshly ground **black pepper**, to taste	

Preheat the oven to 400°F.

Sift the flour and baking powder into a food processor fitted with the plastic blade and season with a little freshly ground black pepper.

In a bowl, beat well together the ricotta, egg, herbs, tomatoes, and milk. Add this cheese mixture to the flour in the food processor and beat to make a soft dough.

Turn out the dough onto a lightly floured surface. Roll it out to form a rough 9-inch circle. (Cut your dough shapes now, if you want.) Place the dough circle or shapes on a baking sheet.

Spread the dough with the tomato paste or Great Tomato Sauce, sprinkle with the olives, and sprinkle the chopped mozzarella over the top.

Bake for 25 minutes, until the cheese is golden and bubbling.

Create your own

Can I help?

Mini chefs will love to roll out the dough and then use their favorite shape cutters to make their own personalized pizzas. They can help with the cheese sprinkling, too.

Toppings to try

- Bell pepper strips
- Ham
- Mushrooms
- Grated zucchini
- Fresh pineapple
- Cooked sliced eggplant
- Sun-dried tomatoes
- Canned tuna
- Cooked shrimp
- Cooked chicken (try some teriyaki chicken)
- Corn kernels
- Olives
- Cooked egg
- Cooked sausage
- Chocolate + banana

The sight, sound, and smell of food sizzling on the BBQ is one of summer's great delights. Children will love to be involved in the grilling process, with careful supervision. Little hands also make light work of kebab preparations, wrapping food in foil and mixing salads and sauces.

Inside-out burgers

makes **8** · prep **15** minutes · cook **5** minutes

1 pound **ground chuck beef**

3 tablespoons finely chopped **flat-leaf parsley**

1 tablespoon **whole-grain mustard**

8 slices **Swisss**, **Gruyère**, or **American cheese**

8 small **whole-wheat hamburger buns**, to serve

Arugula leaves and **tomato** slices, to serve

Freshly ground **black pepper**

Place the ground beef in a bowl, add the parsley and mustard, season well with plenty of freshly ground black pepper, and mix well with a fork.

Divide the mixture into eight equal pieces. Break each piece in half and shape each half into a thin patty. Top one of the patties with a slice of cheese (the cheese should sit within the patty with at least a ½-inch border around it—shape the meat into a larger patty, if necessary). Place the other patty over the top and press down around the edges to secure the cheese inside. Prepare the rest of the patties in the same way.

Cook the burgers on a wire rack over the hot coals for 4–5 minutes on each side, until colored and cooked through.

Serve the burgers in whole-wheat buns with arugula leaves and tomato slices.

181

Sticky sausages

serves 4–6 | prep 5 minutes | cook 10–12 minutes

12 good-quality **small sausages** or **frankfurters**

1 tablespoon **olive oil**

For the glaze

3 tablespoons **honey**

2 tablespoons **whole-grain mustard**

2 tablespoons finely chopped **flat-leaf parsley**

Freshly ground **black pepper**

Place the sausages on a wire rack over the hot coals and cook them for 10–12 minutes, turning them until they are browned all over and cooked through. Remove the sausages from the heat and cut each sausage in half if you wish.

Place the honey, whole-grain mustard, and parsley in a large bowl and mix well, seasoning with a little freshly ground black pepper. Add the hot sausages to the bowl and toss them to coat them in the glaze.

Serve the coated sausages in a bowl and give everyone toothpicks or small forks to prevent sticky fingers. They are delicious accompanied with sticks of carrot, red bell pepper, and celery.

Tasty, buttery corn on the cob

serves 4 | prep 5 minutes | cook 12 minutes

4 cobs fresh **corn**

4 tablespoons **unsalted butter**, slightly softened

1 teaspoon **paprika**

1 tablespoon finely chopped **flat-leaf parsley**

Cut each cob in half. Bring a large saucepan of lightly salted water to the boil and blanch the cobs for 5 minutes. Remove them from the pan.

Cook the blanched cobs on a wire rack over the hot coals for 6–7 minutes, until they are lightly charred and tender.

Meanwhile place the butter in a small mixing bowl with the paprika and parsley and mix well. Place the cobs on serving plates and divide pats of the flavored butter among them, letting the butter melt all over. Serve immediately.

Crunchy veggie kebabs

1 **zucchini**, halved lengthwise and cut into chunks

1 small **orange bell pepper**, seeded and cut into chunks

1 small **red bell pepper**, seeded and cut into chunks

8 **cremini mushrooms**, halved

2 tablespoons **olive oil**

For the glaze

1 tablespoon **ketchup** or **Great Tomato Sauce** (see page 32)

1 tablespoon **honey**

1 teaspoon **Dijon mustard**

Divide the prepared vegetables evenly among eight well-soaked bamboo skewers or eight metal skewers, threading them on in a repeating pattern. Lightly brush each kebab with the oil.

Cook the kebabs on a wire rack over the hot coals for 5–6 minutes, turning occasionally, until the vegetables are lightly charred in places and tender.

Meanwhile make the glaze. Mix together the ketchup or Great Tomato Sauce, honey, and mustard.

Remove the kebabs from the heat and lightly brush them with the glaze.

Banana chocolate treasure

 serves **4** prep **10** minutes cook **10-12** minutes

4 ripe **bananas**

¼ cup **light corn syrup**

4 ounces **semisweet chocolate**, coarsely chopped

½ teaspoon **ground cinnamon**

Vanilla ice cream, to serve (optional)

Slit each banana in half along its length. Place each banana half on a piece of aluminum foil large enough to wrap it up.

Before you wrap, drizzle each length of banana with ½ tablespoon of the corn syrup, then sprinkle each with a little of the chopped chocolate. Finish with a sprinkle of the cinnamon.

Wrap the banana lengths, scrunching up the foil and leaving a small air pocket at the top of each package to let out the steam.

Place the foil-wrapped bananas on a wire rack over the hot coals and cook for 10–12 minutes, until the bananas are soft and the sauce is hot.

Serve with a spoonful of vanilla ice cream (if using).

Fruity mallow kebabs

serves **4** | prep **10** minutes | cook **1** minute

1 slightly underripe **banana**, cut into chunks

8 **strawberries**, hulled

½ firm **mango**, pitted and cut into chunks

8 **marshmallows**

½ teaspoon **cinnamon**

Divide the fruit and marshmallows among four soaked bamboo skewers or four metal skewers.

Place the kebabs on a wire rack over the hot coals and cook for 20–30 seconds on each side, until the marshmallows start to go soft and gooey (don't let them cook too long or they will melt completely).

Sprinkle the cinnamon over the kebabs and serve immediately, while the marshmallows are still soft.

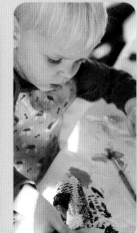

Index

Thank you

A big thank you to all of the Ella's Kitchen employees and friends who contributed recipes for this book and "road tested" them with their own families.

A special thank you to all our little helpers—and their parents and carers—for their patience in front of the camera. Here's a list of our little stars and their ages on the days of our photo shoots:

Adam Bennett (age 3)
Alexander Rogoff (age 3)
Amélie Fricker (age 4)
Amélie Holladay (age 3)
Anna Thomas (age 3)
Annabelle Wilson (age 5)
Ava Di Palma (age 2)
Bella Douglas (age 2)
Ben Fleming (age 2)
Bruce Feng (age 5)
Callum McDonnell (age 1)
Carys Davies (age 3)
Charlie Douglas (age 4)

Charlie Newman (age 18 months)
Chloe Dale (age 3)
Conor Rennard (age 2)
Daisy Hawke (age 2)
Dan Heskia (age 5)
Daniel Woods (age 2)
Dhruv Reddi (age 2)
Dylan Standen (age 2)
Elodie Ramus (age 18 months)
Emily Preddy (age 3)
Emma Clements (age 3)
Ethan Wilson (age 7)
Finley Mason (19 months)
Florence Partridge (20 months)
George Hawke (age 4)
Harrison Slaughter (age 2)
Jackson Brooks-Dutton (age 2)
Jessica Brahams (age 3)
Keeley Carson (age 2)
Marnie Clew (age 2)
Michaela Bruce (age 4)
Millie Roxburgh (age 4)
Noah Quinn (age 3)
Olivia O'Brien (age 4)
Olivia Thaw (age 3)

Ollie Woodall (age 3)
Otis Lindsay (age 3)
Parisa A Sadique (age 2)
Poppy Kelly (age 1)
Poppy Nightingale (age 2)
Rosie Beverley (age 2)
Sam Hullis (age 4)
Sebastian Chippindale-Vives (age 2)
Sofia Walker (age 2)
Theo Hendry (age 2)
Tom Crickmay Rack (age 2)
Tyler Thaw (age 4)
Xanthe Grayburn (age 2)

For letting us take photos at their homes, for providing recipe inspiration, and all of the other important stuff that was needed to make our very first cookbook:

Vanessa Bird, Michelle Bowen, Lee Faber, Nicki Harrold, Catherine Hullis, Alison Lindley, Anita Mangan, Mikha Mekler, Jane Middleton, Victoria Millar

Stickers!

Stars and hearts for the recipes you love
and more to decorate your pages!

yummy!

I cooked this!

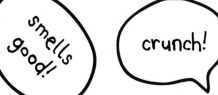

smells good!

crunch!

squashy

delicious

my favorite

mmmmm!

I cooked this for

I cooked this for

I cooked this for

high 5!

high 5!

high 5!

high 5!